A Missionary Journey

Remembering His Marvelous Works

Joan Tyson

A Missionary Journey

Copyright © 2009 by Joan Tyson

All rights reserved. No part of this book may be reproduced or transmitted in any form or by any means without written permission of the author.

ISBN 978-1-61623-895-7

This book is written in memory of someone without whom this book could not have been written. Without God's divine call upon his life and his faithfulness to the Lord in spite of all the odds against him, there would be neither marvelous works nor **"A Missionary Journey"** in our lives to remember and to share with you.

That very special someone is Bob Tyson, who was my husband and my best friend, for 53 years. I dedicate this book in his memory and my prayer is that it will touch someone's heart not to be afraid to start on a missionary journey with the Lord.

To Stephany, my granddaughter (and angel)
God sent you into my life 19 years ago, bringing a joy that only grandmas can understand. I never had a sister nor a daughter, but God sent the best when He sent you to me. When the Lord took "Grandpa" to heaven, you were with me and you have been with me throughout the happy times and the lonely times. You made me so happy when you received Jesus as your Saviour, and you have made me a very proud "grandma" when you said you wanted to be a missionary and take my place one day. You will be a great missionary because you have a heart for missions and missions are in the heart of God.

To Philip and Stevie,
For your dedication to the Lord and your zeal to carry on the work that your dad started many years before either one of you were ever born, I am thankful to the Lord and so proud to be called "Mama" by two such wonderful sons.

To Philip, Jr., Michael, Ashley, Brianna, and Brandon,
I waited for a long time before the Lord sent me your dads, but it was well worth the wait to have grandchildren such as you. My heart's desire is that each one of you will receive Jesus in your hearts at an early age, give your lives to him so that one day **"The Missionary Journey"** that began in the lives of your grandpa and me will continue.

Also to all those who have loved us, prayed for us, and supported us for so many years and who have pleaded with us to **"write it down"** before we get so old we'll forget all the beautiful experiences God has given to us.

THIS BOOK IS LOVINGLY DEDICATED TO ALL OF YOU.

Preface

Over forty-five years have passed since that night when the missionary asked the question, "**Would you be willing to go anywhere at any time and do anything that God would have you to go and do?**"

I had a choice that night, when Bob came home and told me that we were selling out and following God. I could have said, "No, I will never give up my house, my family, my friends, the land your dad gave to us." Yes, I had a choice.

We were not newlyweds. We had been married for eleven years. We were blessed to own our home. We both had good jobs. All of a sudden to give all of this up to go to a foreign country? We had scarcely been out of Georgia. **But the choice was mine.**

In Mark 10:29-30, Jesus said: **"There is no man that hath left house, or brethren, or sisters, or father, or mother, or wife, or children, or lands for my sake, and the gospel's, But he shall receive an hundredfold now in this time, houses, and brethren, and sisters, and mothers, and children and lands, with persecutions; and in the world to come eternal life."**

I didn't even know this verse was in the Bible. I didn't make the choice to go to be able to "get" something in return. God put such a love and desire in my heart to go that I would have gladly paid Him if I could have!

Had I said **"no,"** I shudder to think what I would have missed. I gave up my mom and dad, whom I loved with all my heart; but what did God give me in return?

A family: God gave me a **beautiful family** once we reached foreign soil. Having lost all hope of ever having a child of my own, God gave me two sons. The first one, Philip, was born nine months after reaching foreign soil, after fifteen years of marriage. Steve was born four years later.

They, in turn, have given us two beautiful daughters-in-law, and six beautiful grandchildren.

Houses: God has given us houses, lands, church buildings, feeding centers, schools, and mission centers all over Honduras and Nicaragua. That little house and eight acres of land that we gave up seem mighty small compared to all the things that God has entrusted to our care.

Children: I begged God for years to give me **"just one" child.** Besides giving me a family of my very own, He has given me hundreds and hundreds of little children to love and help. I would never have had the blessing of seeing all these little lives changed but by Jesus´ love.

Friends: What about all the thousands of **friends** He has given to us? We had only a few friends forty-five years ago; now we have thousands.

Had I said "no," I would have missed sharing with you our "**MISSIONARY JOURNEY**" and all the marvelous works of God.

Don't ever be afraid to trust God. Don't think of what you might have to give up if you follow God; **think of what you might be giving up if you don't!**

Table of Contents

1. The Call 1
2. The Good Samaritan 7
3. Impossible With Man; Possible With God 11
4. Snuffyville 17
5. On Our Way 19
6. Learning the Spanish Language 23
7. Our Miracle in Costa Rica 25
8. Nicaragua, the Land of Our Calling 31
9. Palacagüina, Nicaragua 35
10. Gospel Preached From Village To Village 39
11. The First Funeral 43
12. Pueblo Nuevo, Nicaragua 47
13. Tragedy At The Bible Institute 51
14. Bob's Fight With The Demon 55
15. A Year Of Blessings And A Year Of Suffering 59
16. "Just Play Dead" 63
17. God's Mercies 65
18. "And That Your Fruit Should Remain" 69
19. Without Shame 71
20. Teaching Faithful Men 73
21. El Coral 75
22. "Who Shall Separate Us From The Love Of Christ?" ... 79
23. Light Of The Jungle 83

24. Sleeping With The Spiders 87

25. God's Protection 93

26. Stranded In Mexico 97

27. House In Georgia 101

28. Mission Center Taken Over By Sandinistas 105

29. Run Out Of Honduras 109

30. Work Begins In Honduras 111

31. Resident Missionaries In Honduras 115

32. The Man In The Cage 117

33. Another War In Nicaragua 121

34. Marriages In Honduras 123

35. Feed The Hungry 127

36. God's Work Continues Under Communism 133

37. Opportunity Of A Lifetime 135

38. Christian Grammar School 139

39. Christian High School 141

40. Growing For Jesus 145

41. Artesian Well 147

42. Radio Ministry 151

43. Water In Marcovia, Honduras 157

44. Hurricane Mitch 161

45. Another Miracle Of God 163

46. A Year of Growth and Change 165

47. "Via De Victoria" Tabernacle Dedication 169

48. The Prodigal Son Comes Home 173

49. Walking Through The Valley Of The Shadow Of Death 177

50. "Boast Not Thyself Of Tomorrow" 181
51. Missionary Journeys 185
52. "Grace Annex" Grammar School Extension 191
53. Bob's Health 195
54. Showers Of Blessings 199
55. "Home-Going" Of Bob Tyson 203
56. The Trials And Tragedies 209
57. A Man Sent From God 213
58. Conclusion 217

1. The Call

"Ye, have not chosen me, but I have chosen you, and ordained you, that you should go and bring forth fruit, and that your fruit should remain: that whatsoever you shall ask of the Father in my name, he may give it you." —John 15:16

God's missionary call came to us many years ago—in November 1964. The Holy Spirit touched Bob's heart as he heard Brother Frank Rosser, a missionary returning from the field of Nicaragua, speak of the hundreds of towns and villages that had never heard the Gospel.

On that Sunday afternoon, as he was leaving the radio station where he had a weekly program, Bob felt impressed to visit the Grace Baptist Church in Atlanta (formerly known as Cabaggetown) to hear our former pastor, Brother Garland Odom, preach. He asked his friend, Brother Richard Swafford, to go with him. Little did he know this would be a major turning point in his life.

When Bob and Brother Richard entered the church, they saw a man putting up a screen. He introduced himself as Frank Rosser, missionary to Nicaragua. This meant nothing to Bob—he knew nothing about missions. He could not recall ever having seen a missionary.

Bob was born in a Christian home and had heard the Bible preached by his dad all his young life: however, it wasn't until 1958, while on guard duty at a military base in New Jersey, that Bob received the Lord as his personal Saviour. The Holy Spirit convicted him of his sins that night in a guard shack. He knew he was a lost sinner on his way to Hell. His life completely changed that night.

As Frank Rosser began to preach, Bob knew immediately that this was a different message. He had never heard anything like this before. Were there really towns and villages in northern Nicaragua without one gospel-preaching church, not even one Bible? In the slides he saw people who had dragged up old pieces of wood and tin and asked Brother Frank to stay there and build a church for them. He wasn't able to stay, but he promised them that he would send someone back to help. That was his mission that night at Grace Baptist Church. **"Would you be willing to go anywhere at any time and do anything that God would have you to go and do?"** These words touched the very heart and soul of Bob Tyson who, at age thirty, was hearing a missionary for the very first time.

Before Bob could get this settled in his heart, the missionary came out with the next statement: **"If you are not willing to go anywhere at any time and do anything that God would ask of you, then God can't use you!"**

Oh, but Bob wanted to be used by God, and here were people begging for a preacher and a church.

With head bowed and the crack in the hardwood floor seemingly trying to swallow him up, he began to pray. His mental picture of a missionary was someone in a styrofoam hat and Bermuda shorts in a jungle, going to do something (he didn't know what). He also saw himself falling out of a boat in a river deep in the jungles and being eaten by piranhas.

That night he became willing to go to those jungles, and even be eaten by the piranhas, if that was God's will for his life. His hand was raised, signifying that he would go.

After talking with the missionary that night, he came home and woke me up. I'll never forget his words: "Honey, our lives will never be the same after tonight."

I sat up in bed and asked, "Why?"

"Tonight I surrendered to be a missionary!"

"What does that mean?" I asked with excitement.

"It means we're selling everything we have and we're going for God."

We had never heard of Nicaragua—did not even know the country existed. Remember, this was before the computer or the Internet, and the world was a lot bigger in 1964. We were just two insignificant people, raised in a small town, and we had never traveled anywhere.

Oh, how little we knew that night of what was ahead! We were so excited! How wonderfully exciting to embark on a journey with the Lord! All material things lost their value and importance. We were blessed to have our own home paid for by the time we were both twenty-one years old, and Bob's dad had given us eight acres of "family land." Our house didn't mean anything to us anymore. We only saw it as a means to get to northern Nicaragua to tell the people about Jesus.

We thought we would sell our house and immediately go to Nicaragua, but after talking with the missionary, we found that we needed to go to Bible college. We were not counting on this! We had heard all our lives that God called preachers and *He*, **not a seminary,** gave the messages. But if we were going to get to these people, we had to listen to the missionary.

As we look back, we see God's hand directing in our situation. Brother Frank arranged for us to meet him in Chattanooga the following Saturday, and he would go with us to Tennessee Temple University there. We had no idea where we were going or what Tennessee Temple was. We only knew that God had put a burning desire in our hearts to tell others about Jesus. We wanted others to have the peace and joy that we had from knowing our Saviour.

Looking out our window in Villa Rica, Georgia on Saturday morning, we saw a blanket of snow already on the ground and more falling. We had plans to go to Chattanooga, and always the weather gets worse the further north one goes. "Are we going to try to go?" I asked Bob.

"We're going to start out," he said. "If God wants this, He will open up the way."

A few miles up the road the snow vanished. God wanted us to go. We felt the Holy Spirit when we first put our feet on the sidewalk in front of the registration office of Tennessee Temple University. We were introduced to Dr. J. R. Faulkner, assistant pastor of Highland Park Baptist Church and vice president of Tennessee Temple Schools. When he heard our story, he simply bowed his head and said, "Praise God!" This was in December 1964, and before we left there that day, we were registered for the second semester to begin in January 1965—less than three weeks to quit our jobs, sell our house and start a brand-new life!

Our plans were to sell our home and land, pay our way through school, get part-time jobs and breeze through with no problems. But God had other plans for us. We needed to learn to trust Him, not our bank account!

A flaw was found in the landline of our deed, and we needed Bob's mother to give us a new deed in order to sell. Bob's dad had already gone to be with the Lord. His mother was a dedicated Christian woman, a preacher's wife. She had traveled with Bob's dad doing home missionary work, but she just couldn't understand why we would go to a foreign land when "there's enough to do right here."

She refused to make us a new deed. Her land joined ours. All of this was "family land."

In the meantime, we sold our television, stereo and other things and left for Tennessee Temple. We didn't understand what God was doing at that time, but looking back, we now see it all clearly. We had never really lived by faith. We knew we were saved by faith, but our daily living depended on our checkbooks. God had some lessons ahead for us.

It came to a point that if we ate, it was because God sent us the food.

I will never forget a pastor and student, Dewey Roberts. On Fridays he went to his church about sixty miles from Chattanooga. On Monday mornings, he would bring us cracked eggs and dark hamburger meat that one of the members of his church had left over from his store.

This was forty-five years ago, yet it seems like yesterday. We experienced God's provision over and over again. No matter how little it was, we knew that it came from Him!

Bob tells the story about going to his job after classes one day in a car that belonged to the delivery company where he worked. He had one dime in his pocket. In 1965 one dime would buy a Jiffy hamburger. He stopped at a Jiffy restaurant and spent that dime. He was so hungry that he had his Jiffy eaten before he even got back to the car. A voice told him to get out of the car, get the dime that was on the running board and buy another hamburger. It seemed foolish to listen to that voice, but he did. Sure enough, there was a beautiful, shiny dime that looked brand-new. He took it, ran back to the little café and said, "Praise God! Give me another hamburger!"

A few months before God called us, Bob had bought me a brand-new red 1964 Ford convertible—a beautiful car. That one luxury we didn't even think about taking to Chattanooga. It was left on the car lot of Gibbs Motor Company in Austell, Georgia to be resold. Those car payments were eighty-eight dollars a month! We were able to make three payments after moving to Chattanooga; then there was absolutely no money to make another.

I knelt by my bed and asked God please to help us with that car. "Lord, what kind of testimony are we going to have, studying to be missionaries, when we cannot even pay our bills?"

Would you believe that in just a few days we had a letter from Hugh and Mamie Gibbs saying they knew we must be having problems trying to make the car payments. They had gotten in touch with the bank, and the bank had said we only had to keep up the interest until the car sold. Hugh and Mamie Gibbs said they had already paid three months of interest for us.

The convertible sold in June. Had I prayed earlier, I wonder if it would have saved us three months' car payments! We were learning to *ask* and *receive* from our Heavenly Father.

Several months passed while we were learning to trust our Lord before He allowed Bob's mother to make us a new deed. One might say she was not a very good Christian, but she was a wonderful Christian who was just obeying the Lord. Had we gone into training with lots of money, perhaps we would never have learned to trust the Lord.

Now for forty-five years we have trusted Him to supply all our needs, and He has done it, just as He did in our early days of training!

In God's time our house sold, as did everything else we had left behind, but nothing sold until God taught us a great lesson: we were no longer to trust anyone or anything else for our survival—only Him.

"I have chosen you, and ordained you, that ye should go and bring forth fruit, and that your fruit should remain: that whatsoever ye shall ask of the Father in my name, he may give it you." —John 15:16

2. The Good Samaritan

Luke 10:30-37

Studying at Tennessee Temple Bible College could be compared to sitting down to a delicious feast every day. We had never experienced anything like this before. Studying under godly men like Dr. Lee Roberson, Dr. J. R. Faulkner, Dr. Bruce Lackey, Dr. Clyde Paul White, filling our hearts daily with the Word of God and growing in the Lord Jesus Christ made us feel that we were experiencing a little bit of heaven on earth.

But hearing the Word of God day after day, learning how to win souls but not putting it into practice made us feel as if we were doing nothing for the Lord.

One day Bob walked into Dr. Faulkner's office and said, "Dr. Faulkner, I feel as if I'm drying up."

"You're not drying up, Bob," remarked Dr. Faulkner. "You're about to explode. You need to start giving out what you've learned."

A few weeks later found us seventy-five miles away in Sherwood, Tennessee, in one of the Highland Park's chapels. Sherwood was an old limestone-mining town. The limestone mines had been shut down years before, leaving a town filled with people with no jobs. And there were many illiterates. Bootlegging was common, and moonshine flowed freely. Since there was no law in the town, men did what they thought was right in their own eyes. The place was filled with suffering, hungry and abused children. Many of them were abandoned.

We rented an old, abandoned Methodist church building. We spent all day Saturday, before our first service on Sunday, scrubbing soot (caused by the pot-bellied stove that sat in the middle of the floor) from the walls and floor.

The first Sunday five people were present, including Bob and me. Someone had put a dead dog under the church. This was our "welcome" to Sherwood.

It was not unusual to hear gunfire on Saturday nights as we lay on a mattress on the floor of the little three-room cabin we had rented.

We would go to Sherwood as soon as our classes ended on Friday and stay until after service on Sunday night. We visited up and down the hollows in this forsaken mountain town, but all we had learned in our Bible classes on winning people to the Lord—the Romans road of salvation—just didn't seem to be working for us.

One night Bob was walking down a trail. Looking up toward Heaven, he cried out, "O God, what am I doing in this terrible place? What can I do? It will take a better preacher than I am to do a work here."

Immediately the parable of the Samaritan came to his mind. Sherwood could be compared to the man who had fallen by the wayside, left wounded and half dead with no one to bind up his wounds. Everyone had walked on by, ignoring the suffering, the wounded, the sin-sick. God in His mercy had sent us to Sherwood to be the Samaritan.

Our lives and ministry took a dramatic turn. On Sunday mornings Bob was out literally "running down" his congregation, while I waited in the cabin heating water to wash the filth off little children who had been living in their own filth for a week. Many of the children were like little animals. They lived in freezing temperatures with no heat. Their parents were somewhere, drunk. The children would run when they saw Bob coming, but once he had them inside the little Volkswagen, they became calm. I would literally have to peel off their clothes. And the smell was awful!

Students at Tennessee Temple gave clothes for the children, but the demand was greater than the supply, since every week we were burning the old clothes and putting on the new ones.

When the Jaycees of Cobb County, Georgia, headed up by our dear friends, Hugh and Mamie Gibbs, brought up Christmas toys to our mission, an article about our work with a picture was put in the newspaper. A short time later, a letter was received from Attorney L. S. Cobb from Marietta, Georgia, asking if there was any way he could help us. I quickly wrote back that we needed a washing machine to wash the children's clothes, explaining the situation with the children but adding that just a secondhand wringer washing machine would do.

Lawyer Cobb hastily replied: "I am a saved Methodist, and I've been looking for ways to clean up the Baptists! A new Kenmore automatic washing machine is on its way to you."

When Good Samaritan Baptist Missions, Inc., was chartered in 1973, it was Lawyer Cobb who did all the legal work—free of charge! He remained a good friend until God called him Home.

On Saturday nights in Sherwood, our little cabin became a refuge for the hungry and weary. Children were fed (God miraculously provided the food). Old people began to come, many just to have someone to talk to. What beautiful memories of all the singing, the laughter, the children playing! Always we were sure to tell them about the love of Jesus.

On Sundays, the little church began to fill, and the singing could be heard up and down the hollows of Sherwood, Tennessee. The little three-room cabin soon became too small. A large eight-room mission house was made available to us. Soon furniture, clothing and food were being received from all over the United States to help these dear people.

God also sent a precious family to help us in Sherwood—George and Anne Westbrook and their children. George was also a student at Tennessee Temple. Anne blessed our hearts as she played the piano in the little church with George leading the music—and I still remember those delicious cakes she would bake and bring on Sunday. Their love for the

Lord was so evident in the way they loved the people of Sherwood, Tennessee.

Every Sunday, there was a baptism in the river of Sherwood. People as old as ninety-four years were baptized. Every weekend Highland Park Baptist Church in Chattanooga sent ordained ministers to baptize.

One day Dr. Faulkner said, "Bob, fill out papers for your ordination." Bob had only been at Tennessee Temple for six months. The usual requirement for ordination from Highland Park Baptist Church was to finish seminary. Bob, who had not even studied Bible doctrines, had to go before an ordination council of doctors of theology! The Highland Park Baptist Church ordained Bob Tyson on October 28, 1965, giving their approval and expressing their confidence in the call of God upon his life.

For three and one-half years, God let us labor in Sherwood. A book in itself could be written on the glorious experiences that He gave us there. So many elderly people, living back in the mountains, heard the Gospel and received the Lord Jesus Christ. What joy to see lives and homes changed and abandoned children reunited with parents!

3. Impossible With Man; Possible With God

Matthew 19:26

We saw many miracles during our ministry in Sherwood. God was teaching and training Bob and Joan Tyson for our work in years ahead on the foreign mission fields, teaching us this great truth from His Word: "With men this is impossible; but with God all things are possible."

Before leaving this chapter in our lives, we share with you an experience that has blessed thousands of hearts. It is the story of our dear, dear brother in Christ, Bill Will Garner of Sherwood.

Bill Will was the number one moonshiner in Franklin County, Tennessee. Bob met him one day as he was walking through town inviting people to church. He asked Bob to come to his house and visit. Bob went on several occasions, but always Bill Will would run or hide when he saw him coming.

One Sunday morning after service, Bob asked Brother Meek, one of the brothers of the church whom God had miraculously saved and given a new life (he'd been married five times!), to go with him to visit Bill Will Garner. "We'll catch him while he is eating lunch," said Bob, "and he won't be able to run from us."

They drove over to Bill Will's cabin. Bob went to the back door, and Brother Meek went to the front door. Bob stepped into the doorway and surprised all the family as they were eating their Sunday meal. He took out his little New Testament and began to preach.

Bill Will rose from the table, walked past Bob and on around to the front porch. Bob followed and approached him with these words: "Mr. Garner, wouldn't you like to give your heart to the Lord today?"
"Yep, I believe I would," replied Bill Will.

Bob and Bill Will knelt there on the front porch of that little cabin, and Bill Will talked to God in his mountain terminology—a prayer Bob says he wishes he had recorded.

Bill Will got up off his knees with a radiance on his face and peace in his heart.

Bob asked, "What happened, Mr. Garner?"

"The Lord has saved me," Bill Will replied.

Bob encouraged him to tell someone about it. Quickly he raced back into the kitchen to tell his family that he had received the Lord Jesus into his heart.

Bill Will had a "steel" (still) in the woods, but instead of running off more liquor, he called the sheriff and told him to come and "cut the 'steel' down."

Weeks passed. Bill Will's testimony was now known throughout the county. His baptism drew many of his ex-customers, who said, "We won't believe it until we see it!"

Now Bill Will's income had stopped, and there was no work to be found. (In the mid-sixties there was no welfare in that part of the country.) Bill Will was in trouble! He had a large family to feed; a lot of grandchildren lived in his house.

We wondered what would happen to him. Would he get discouraged and return to his old trade? **The little church began to pray.**

One Friday as we entered Sherwood, we were met by one of Bill Will's grandsons. He was very excited. We could barely understand him, but we did hear the words "Train wreck—Papa's house." We went as fast as our little Volkswagen would take us up the hollow. But as we came into view of the wreck, all we could see was a mountain of corn! Bill Will's cabin was built alongside the railroad track, and four boxcars of shelled corn had overturned into his yard.

Bob made his way around the boxcars and through the corn. In his overalls, his suit coat and black felt hat, Bill Will was looking over the situation.

"What in the world happened?" Bob asked.

"A train wrecked," answered Bill Will. He picked up some corn, shook it around in his hand, threw it down and very calmly said, "They gave me a job."

"Doing what?" asked Bob

"Guarding the corn," said Bill. Guarding the corn in his own yard at fifty dollars a week! That was *good* money in 1965!

After several weeks of mending the tracks, gathering up all the wreckage and saving what corn they could, the railroad asked Bill if he could use the rest of the corn. (Several inches were left on the ground so as not to mix dirt and corn together.) "Yep, I believe we can," replied Bill.

So Bill, his wife and daughters sacked up bushels of corn. They had so much corn that Brother Red (known as the town's ex-drunk whom the Lord had miraculously saved) stood in church one Sunday morning and, with tears in his eyes, asked the church to pray for Brother Bill Will. "He's got a tolerable lot of corn. And you know what you do with corn, don't you?"

Well, neither Brother Red nor the church had anything to worry about, because Bill Will didn't go back to making liquor. He sold corn everywhere and rejoiced in the way God had provided for him.

Not long after, Bob visited with Bill Will's wife who had recently been saved. She told Bob how God had sent in a *second load*. "I was standing on the porch watching the 'Ole Niner' go by. [They had all of the trains named.] Corn suddenly began to splatter up to my feet. God had sent us the second load." The same thing had happened again in the very same place.

Bob talked to the foreman of the railroad who said, "Preacher, we have a problem here. We can't get a corn car to pass this place." God was providing for an old moonshiner who had given it all up for the Lord. This was a mission impossible—**impossible with man but not impossible with God!**

Brother Garner remained faithful to the Lord. By this time most of his family had been saved. On a Saturday morning, Bob went by to see Bill Will while on visitation. He always wanted the preacher to come and "sit a spell" with him. While they were warming by the fire, Bill arose and, taking two coal buckets in his hand, said, "Wait a minute, Preacher. I'll be right back."

Bob waited and waited. Finally he looked out the window and saw him coming over the tracks with two large buckets of "big" coal.

"Where did you get that coal, Bill?" Bob asked suspiciously.

"O Preacher, I forgot to tell you about the seven boxcars of coal that turned over the other day on the other side of the tracks."

Isn't that just like God—putting the shelled corn in Bill Will's freshly swept yard but putting the sooty coal on the other side of the tracks!

If I keep going with this story, you will think I'm lying but I'm not! All of this happened in the life of a moonshiner who had the sheriff come and cut down his "steel" in the woods after he got saved!

A few months later, a tractor trailer loaded with fresh green beans, covered by a canvas top, was making its way down the winding mountain road from Sewanee to Sherwood—one of the most crooked roads in the world. The driver had come around all the curves and was now on the straight way and seemed to have it made. All of a sudden the trailer jackknifed and overturned. The beans came rushing down the side of the mountain and piled up on the pine straw at the back of Bill Will's barn!

Several men from the trucking company, slipping and sliding, tried unsuccessfully to carry the beans back up the mountain. At last the owner came by and gave the order to leave them there: "It just isn't worth the effort."

"Can you use these beans, Mister?" he asked Bill Will, who was standing there with his wife and daughters.

"Yep, I believe I can," he answered.

Bill and his family sold beans all over town. And Mrs. Garner canned so many green beans that they still had jars of them at their death!

Several years ago God gave us the opportunity to return to Sherwood. We went to the place by the side of the railroad tracks where Bill Will Garner's cabin once stood. As we stood there, memories came rushing back.

Thank You, God, for giving Bob and me all of these precious memories. Thank You, God, for teaching us here in this place that You can do anything. Nothing is impossible with You, Lord. Thank You for saving Bill Will Garner. Thank You for all the cottage prayer meetings we had in the little cabin here by the side of the railroad tracks. Thank You for his testimony. And thank You, Lord, for allowing Bob and me to be Good Samaritans in Sherwood, Tennessee.

4. Snuffyville

Our time in Sherwood came to an end in September 1967. God was once again turning our hearts to northern Nicaragua and we were anxious to get started. We needed six more months to graduate from Tennessee Temple and we needed to start thinking about raising support....

Once again, God sent Frank Rosser into our lives when one day he approached Bob and asked him if there was any way he could go to a little mission he had started in the outskirts of Summerville, Georgia. This place was called Snuffyville and was just as bad as its name. The jail in Summerville was mostly filled with people from Snuffyville—drugs and liquor flowed freely. Bob immediately said he would go. I am thinking, "But I thought we were going to spend this time in preparation to leave for Nicaragua", but I knew better than to say anything negative. I had complete confidence in God's call upon Bob's life, something I never doubted, and if he was going to Snuffyville, wherever it was, then I would go too.

On our first visit to Snuffyville, I was disappointed. It was so different than Sherwood. *How can I ever get close to these people*, I thought. I remember our first service in a house there. A young girl stumbled in the room, obviously on drugs or drunk with liquor. She didn't like something Bob said, jerked her wig off, threw it on the floor and walked out bald. Someone said she had shaved her head while drunk.

Welcome to Snuffyville!!! "Lord, is this where you want us for our last few months in the United States?"

Bob knew he had to have help so it was announced in chapel at Tennessee Temple that he needed some dedicated students to help him in Snuffyville. **And God sent the best....**This was the **"dream team"** of missions...And the little church grew. Every week souls were saved.

This was our mission team...

Richard Comer, who has been a missionary since he finished Tennessee Temple,

Steve Fazekas, ministering for many years with the great mission, Answers in Genesis.

Dale and Sarah Wolery, students at Tennessee Temple, who were single at the time, and later married. Dale is the founder and director of Clergy Recovery Network.

Sarah's sister, Belinda, took care of children in the nursery so mothers could hear the Gospel.

And when time came for us to leave for Nicaragua, George and Ann Westbrook, joined the team to pastor the church that had been raised up.

All of these young people were students at Tennessee Temple and what wonderful, wonderful experiences God gave us together in Snuffyville. Money could never buy these precious memories. So many people were saved...So many lives were changed. There were services every Sunday afternoon in the jail in Summerville and lives were changed there.

And, an everlasting love and friendship developed among all of us who were working in Snuffyville. It was a joy to work with these young people and see the enthusiasm and love they had to win souls for Christ. We are all working in different parts of the world now but the memories remain.

5. On Our Way

Saturday, August 17, 1968, we flew from Miami to Managua, Nicaragua, Central America. What a thrill and blessing at last to see the land where God had called us to go almost four years before. We had finished three and one-half years of study at Tennessee Temple University, going straight through summer school until the last summer before graduation, which we spent living in the mission house in Sherwood with our dear friends.

What wonderful, wonderful memories of that summer in Sherwood that God has left imprinted on our minds: memories like Brother Charlie, over eighty-five years old, already sitting on our front porch when we got up in the morning wanting someone to talk to; Brother Red bringing us fresh fish to eat; Sister Eslick, who was seventy-five when she got saved; Sister Renee, who was close to ninety; and all the children, now so different than when we first met them. Yes, God gave us that last summer to cherish forever.

And the memories are still fresh in our minds of Snuffyville and the young people we left behind to carry on the work there.

Sherwood and Snuffyville were added blessings that God gave to us. When we left Villa Rica, Georgia, we would have never, never dreamed that God would take us to these places and give us on hand "boot camp" training, as Bob used to call it, to prepare us before sending us to the land of our calling.

After spending only three and a half months on deputation, getting promises of approximately $450 a month support, Bob was ready to go. "Those people are dying and going to Hell," he said. "We don't have time to wait around."

So, after saying good-bye to all our dear friends at Sherwood, Snuffyville, and to our families, we were on our way. There were three barrels and a washing machine in the back of our van. Bob had insisted that I could wash our clothes in the river, but he gave in when he saw we did have room in the van for the washing machine.

We drove to Miami, leaving our van there to be shipped to Guatemala, and later picked up and driven to Nicaragua, then on to Costa Rica. The next day Bob and I boarded a plane, leaving our homeland to embark on a journey that God had already mapped out for our next forty-two years!

We were able to spend ten wonderful blessing-filled days in Nicaragua on our way to San José, Costa Rica, to study the Spanish language. I can still feel the thrill of knowing this was where God had called us. In the capital of Managua, Nicaragua, we visited some of the churches that were started by the mission. Although we couldn't speak the language, we were able to give out tracts. Bob took out his guitar everywhere we went, and soon crowds would gather to hear us sing to them in English; then they in turn would sing to us in Spanish. God gave us such a love for those people. We were able to communicate on a limited basis simply by signs and expressions. Some of the people knew just a little English, and with our five or six newly learned Spanish words, we really got along well.

Before services started one night, we visited a family who lived next door to the church and asked them to go to church with us. They refused, saying they had their own religion. As we stood outside talking with them further, the man tried to tell us something by pointing first to Bob's hair, then to the inside of the house. We asked if we could go in.

Inside was a darling little girl with reddish-brown hair. They were so proud that it looked a little like Bob's hair. They showed us around the house, which was very clean in spite of dirt floors and almost no roof. The man proudly showed us his chickens and pigeons roosting in the kitchen and his animal hides on the walls. How sad to see the many false gods and idols that could never bring peace to this man nor to his family!

When we started to leave, much to our surprise they told us they were coming to church too. Quite a number of people were there at the church, and many had to stand in the yard. Everyone was surprised that this devoutly religious family would come with us.

Our last night in Nicaragua, before leaving for San José, Costa Rica, to study Spanish, I remember our singing in English "God Be With You Till We Meet Again." The people quickly recognized the melody of the song and in turn sang to us "He Will Take Care of You."

God did take care of us, and He brought us back to those wonderful people one year later.

6. Learning the Spanish Language

Trying to learn the Spanish language was one of the greatest challenges the Lord had ever given us. Hours were spent in trying to pronounce words that meant absolutely nothing to us. Our classes were very small, and most of the students were not only much younger than we were, but having studied Spanish in high school or college, they began to pick up the language immediately.

Bob and I sat dumbfounded. When the teacher said, "Repita, repita," we didn't know what that meant. Now we know it means "repeat" after her.

One day she became very upset with Bob while trying to get him to repeat after her, "El camion esta descompuesto en el camino." (The truck is broken down on the road.) "Repita, repita," she demanded! She began to hit the desk as she continued.

"Hold it right there, young lady," called out Bob. (She had gotten his red hair stirred up.) "You repeat after me," he said: "diagnostically speaking, my physical equilibrium is not organically acquiescent." This was a phrase Bob's old army buddy, Lou Mangone, had taught him in New York when the soldiers made fun of his Southern talk.

Well, the young Spanish teacher could understand a little English, but she couldn't get a hold of that. Afterwards she and Bob became friends, and she exercised a little more patience!

Another teacher did everything she could to help Bob. She even brought a mirror to the classroom to try to teach him where to put his tongue to pronounce the double *r,* making a little motor sound—a "must" to speak good Spanish, we were told.

Finally, in desperation, she asked in her broken English, "How did you play with your little cars when you were a little boy?"

Hmm, thought Bob, *I never thought it would be important in my ministry how I played with my little cars.* He thought back to the old farmhouse with the front porch built high off the ground, where he made little roads all under the porch to push his little wooden cars. After he thought for a moment, he replied, "Bu-dum, Bu-dum." This was not exactly what the teacher wanted. She wanted him to make the little motor sound. He finally learned how to do it, but it was a long journey.

Every Friday afternoon all the missionaries who were learning Spanish would go to different areas and hold services. Bob's job was to pick the guitar. People would come out of their houses to listen; then a missionary would preach the Gospel. This was a discouraging time for Bob. Only God knew how he wanted to preach His Word, but there was the language barrier. The Devil kept telling him that preaching was an impossibility, that he would never preach in Spanish.

One day he said to me, "Honey, somewhere I made a wrong turn. I will never learn this language." We even made a trip to the country of Panama because we understood English was spoken there. But when we found no peace from God, we sadly returned to Costa Rica. We had absolutely no one to encourage us. Our families in the United States still thought we had made a terrible mistake. Not one missionary would ask Bob to pray in church, afraid that even God wouldn't understand his bad Spanish. It all seemed so hopeless.

But God had not forgotten His servants. He was working in a way that we never, never dreamed could happen to us. A song says, "Don't give up on the brink of a miracle." God was about to perform another miracle in the lives of Bob and Joan Tyson.

7. Our Miracle in Costa Rica

"And Jesus answered and said, Verily I say unto you, There is no man that hath left house, or brethren, or sisters, or father, or mother, or wife, or children, or lands, for my sake, and the gospel's, But he shall receive an hundredfold now in this time." — Mark 10:29-30

Just a few weeks after arriving in Costa Rica, I began to feel very tired—not sick, just tired. When other missionaries went out to the street meetings or to give out tracts, I went to bed. Bob thought I had backslid. The other missionaries thought I had amoebas, a disease caused by the little parasite you get from bad water or food. So it was decided that I should see a doctor. In those days, doctors didn't have nurses, so Bob went in with me and was sitting beside me as the doctor talked and did the examination.

When he began to talk about "suspicion of pregnancy," I quickly replied, "Doctor, I am not pregnant. I can't have children."

"Has someone told you that you can't have children?" he asked.

"No." I said, "but we have been married for over fourteen years, and I can't have children."

"Well," the doctor said, "I am convinced, but I see it is going to take more to convince you. We will run some tests and let you know the results in three days."

Pregnant after fourteen years of marriage? It couldn't be. I must have cancer or some other disease. I dared Bob to tell anyone about this. "We'll be laughed at," I said, "because it can't possibly be true."

I thought of all those years and years I had begged God to give me a baby; then when it didn't happen, I shed many tears. When I saw people with children who didn't even want them, I would think, *O God, if You would just give me one!* But after God called us and gave us all those precious little children in Sherwood and then in Snuffyville, I was reconciled to the fact that He wanted Bob and me to be mom and dad to all the little children who needed someone to love them.

Well, Bob *did* tell all the other missionaries, and all were excited but me.

One of the missionary families was living in a very nice home of a Costa Rican family who had gone to the United States. The house was equipped with a speaker phone, so after three days we all gathered there to call the doctor. Here were his words: "I'm sorry, Mrs. Tyson. There was a problem, and we'll need to run the tests again."

Three days later we all gathered again only to be told this time that this was a new "frog" test and things were going wrong. He needed to make the test again. By this time everyone but me was convinced. Bob, upset from having to take so many urine specimens downtown, warned me that I had better believe because this was the last time.

The third time we called the doctor, he said I was definitely pregnant. I still found it hard to believe, so I said, "When I feel him move, then I will believe."

Well, God let me feel him move on a Saturday afternoon while resting. After feeling a little twitch, I shouted for joy!

Fourteen years of marriage—I would soon be thirty-two and Bob was thirty-four. Now God was giving us our first child. We were reminded of Mark 10:29 and 30: 'You have not left fathers, mothers, brothers, sisters, land, that I will not repay you in this life.'

Who would have thought that God would repay us in this way for *going*? If we could have, we would have repaid him for *calling* us. But that's the way our God is. He fulfills His promises.

After that, when Bob became discouraged and thought he might have made a wrong turn somewhere in following God, I had a fear that if we now turned back, God might take our baby. I was convinced that He was giving us this child because of our obedience to Him. I didn't know what might happen if we gave up or turned aside.

Someone told me about a grammar teacher/preacher named Claudio Rojas, who did tutoring on the side. I asked Claudio if he would tutor Bob. At first he didn't give me much attention, saying only that he had no time. Claudio said later that these words of mine touched his heart: "I know that God has called my husband, and he has to learn Spanish to be able to preach."

The next day Claudio was at our house, and his first words were, "Let's speak in Spanish." After about an hour, he said to Bob, "You don't need any classes; you just need to use what you're already learned." He went on to say, "God has sent you to Costa Rica with His message of salvation. There are too many missionaries coming down here just to sightsee. You need to preach." That was the beginning of a ministry that God gave to Claudio Rojas and Bob. From then on, almost every night Claudio and Bob were found in the streets of San José, Costa Rica, showing Christian films and preaching, many time dodging rocks thrown at them but experiencing God's blessings as never before. Bob has said many times that Claudio Rojas will receive rewards at the judgment seat of Christ for every soul saved in our ministry. Claudio Rojas was sent from God to help Bob Tyson.

We also thank God for Colin and Fran Duncan, who were also studying Spanish and who worked with us in the beginning. Colin had a missionary's heart and a burning desire to see souls saved in Costa Rica. Colin and Fran helped us to buy land in one of the very poor areas of San José. We named it "hog hole" because it was such a dirty place. But the Lord let us see many souls saved there. When we first went there with street meetings, a lady was saved and opened up a room in her attic. We called this the "upper room." Many precious services were held in this upper room.

The Devil fought all the way against our having a church in this place. Rocks were thrown against the house while we were trying to have service. Bob had to pay someone to guard our van. Once, when he was to baptize seventeen people in the river, he stepped off into mud and his feet stuck. Behind him was a large hill, and immediately big boulders were pushed off the hill into the river. The new Christians never moved and never showed fear. From the side of the river, a man who was not even a Christian called out, "Preacher, there is a much better place to baptize just down the river. It's not so muddy there." So Bob and the new Christians joined hands and moved to a safer place, and there they were baptized.

I remember one particular Lord's Supper being served. All the baptized believers knelt around an old table, and each one prayed. What a precious sight to see Sister Rosa, in her sixties and with feet rough and crude from walking for years without shoes, kneeling there asking the Lord to forgive her of any sin in her life and thanking Him for bringing her out of darkness into the true light.

While we were studying Spanish we saw people saved every week. God saw the desires of our heart. He brought us in contact with people who had a hunger in their hearts to know God. Such was the case of José and Carmen, two lost people living together without marriage but with a hunger in their hearts. José and Carmen received the Lord and opened up their little home for services in the neighborhood of San Antonio.

It was in this place that Claudio told Bob, "Brother Bob, get ready. You're going to preach Sunday." Bob preaching in Spanish! *A **mission impossible**,* Bob thought. He didn't think he could do it. He told God that if He wanted him to preach, to please send someone to hear him. It was raining hard that day, so the drunks came in off the street to get out of the rain. They heard Bob preach his first message in Spanish. After the service, one of them came up to Bob and said in broken English, "Preacher, I just wanted you to know that I understood every word you said." That was the beginning of Bob's preaching the Gospel in Spanish.

We didn't get to see the fruit while we were there, but many years ago we returned to San José and looked up José and Carmen. What a blessing it was to see them still living for the Lord and to see a large Central American church in their area. José, one of the leaders in the church, said, "Brother Bob, you wouldn't believe how many men are saved here now."

Many times the Devil tells us we can't do anything. We can't, but God can!

May 27, 1969, nine months after reaching foreign soil, a precious baby boy was laid on my chest at the Bible Clinic in San José, Costa Rica. We named him Philip Ray Tyson after the "missionary" Philip in the Bible who "got up and went." Felipe (his Spanish name) was dedicated to the Lord months before he was born. We named him at that time because Bob just knew he would be a boy. "Lord, make him the missionary that I will never be and give him the Spanish language that is so hard for me." God answered that prayer, and it was our son Philip who built six radio stations in Nicaragua and Honduras. He speaks Spanish like the Latinos and was used by God to build many tall radio towers, which can be seen when visiting the mission field. (I will tell you more about this in a later chapter.)

Our year of language study was a time of working for the Lord. Although Bob would probably have been voted "The one Least Likely to Do Anything for the Lord on the Mission Field," God allowed us to finish our course in Costa Rica. We left there knowing that our time had not been spent in vain.

It was on to Nicaragua, to the place where God had called us. It had been a long road—three and one-half years in Bible school at Tennessee Temple, "boot camp" in Sherwood and Snuffyville, and a year of language study in San José, Costa Rica. Now we were finally going to Nicaragua, to the towns and villages without one Gospel-preaching church, to the place where God had called us some four and a half years ago. We had added to our worldly possessions a baby crib that the missionaries gave us. Then it was Bob, Philip, and I embarking on our next journey of a mission impossible.

8. Nicaragua, the Land of Our Calling

We said good-bye to all our friends in Costa Rica and left for the country of Nicaragua. We rented a house on the southern highway about thirty minutes from Managua, the capital, where we lived until we could get our residence and all the government paperwork done. It was the middle of the rainy season, and the rains were coming down hard. Bob borrowed a tent that would seat about three hundred, and with equipment that we had bought while in Costa Rica, we were anxious to get to work.

In the middle of November 1969, we started a campaign in the new area where land had been given to the thousands who had lost their homes in the heavy rainy season. The first two weeks were filled with trials from Satan. You could see him working in every way to prevent the Gospel from being preached. For example, it was necessary to use a power plant which completely tore up (threw a rod); the projector lens burst while we were showing a filmstrip; two or three nights, just before time for service, the public address equipment refused to work; three times the winds put at least a thirty-foot rip in the tent. On and on I could show you Satan at work. **But the darkest time is always just before the dawn.**

On the fifteenth night of our campaign, God began to bless in a tremendous way. For the next eleven nights we had approximately 2500 in attendance, and forty-three people were saved! In my Bible classes on Wednesday afternoons, averaging ninety-eight in attendance, sixteen children made professions of faith.

In our campaigns we had very little group singing because no one knew Christian songs. We taught them some choruses, then some hymns. Later we started having testimonies from those who had been saved. We would then have a filmstrip on the life of Christ to introduce the message. By the time the message was delivered, the people well understood the message. An invitation was given, and each person who came forward was dealt with personally until his faith was placed firmly in the Word of God.

While the meetings were going on, our little Philip developed a terrible skin rash. The doctor in the capital told us *not* to take Philip around the poor children. When I explained that this was impossible, the doctor said, "At least don't let the people touch him." How could we stop those hundreds of people from putting their hands on our child? Many times as I played the little pump organ, I could see his little white head as he was passed from one person to another. Philip finally got over his skin rash. We never tried to keep him from the people, and we feel this is a good lesson for missionaries today. Don't isolate yourself or your family from those God has called you to serve. We have seen much of this in our ministry. The people never feel close to the missionary who does this.

We saw many people saved during this thirty-night campaign, and a church was raised up.

Always humorous things happen, and certainly these experiences didn't escape us. A national boy who was working with us said, "Brother Bob, you are doing great in your preaching. The people understand everything you say, but you have just one word wrong."

Just one letter in a word made the difference between "knees" and "roller skates." The young preacher said to Bob, "In the invitation you're telling people to come to the Lord on their roller skates instead of knees." Well, the tent was on a hillside; but, of course, "roller skates" was incorrect wording and "knees" was not to be literal. Bob had meant to tell them to come on their knees in humbleness.

That's not the only mistake Bob or I have made in the Spanish language down through the years, but it is one never forgotten because it happened in the first tent meeting. The Spanish people are very polite and would never deliberately show disrespect to a man of God, but there were times when it was hard for them to hold back the laughter.

During this time, we had two young Nicaraguans living with us—Miguel, seventeen years of age, who was recommended to us to help us in the work; and Socorro, also seventeen, who appeared in our yard one day to see if we needed someone to help with Philip. Miguel was Bob's first Bible student, and he taught him daily on our front porch, using his notes and textbooks from Tennessee Temple University. Socorro wasn't saved at the time, but she was later saved in one of our tent meetings. When we left for northern Nicaragua in December of the same year, Miguel and Socorro went with us. Our family was growing. A few years later, they were married and have been in the Lord's work for many years. Miguel is a pastor, and Socorro teaches the children and plays the organ.

9. Palacagüina, Nicaragua

"And let us not be weary in well doing: for in due season we shall reap, if we faint not," —Gal 6:9

January 1970: We started off the new year by opening our first campaign for 1970 in a town called Palacagüina, Nicaragua. Following the plan that Bob felt God had given him and remembering His call to take the Gospel to the towns and villages that had never heard, Bob, Miguel, and Missionary Colin Duncan (who had also left language school in Costa Rica and who already had a national preacher to help him) joined efforts to form an evangelistic team in this campaign.

Bob, Philip, and I slept on the floor of Colin and Fran's apartment for thirty nights during this campaign, never thinking of this as any kind of sacrifice or suffering. These were some of our happiest days, because at last we had reached the towns and villages in northern Nicaragua where God had called us to go.

What a meeting we had in Palacagüina! Riding through the town trying to find someone to help us, we were told, "There are no gospel believers here." We put the tent up on the town plaza but told no one who we were or what we were going to do. Many thought a circus was coming to town. The first night about one hour before the meeting was to start, Bob rode around town and announced the meeting over loudspeakers. By the time he got back to the tent, it was already three-fourths full. We averaged 350 per night. After three weeks there had been twenty-eight professions of faith and twenty-one baptisms.

This was an old western town, filled with cantinas, drunken brawls and gunfights on Saturday nights. But something new had come to town, and everyone wanted to see what it was. Antonio Inestroza, a young lad of fourteen, said his heart was made glad because he thought he would get to see clowns and monkeys after a hard day of hauling creek water to sell door to door to help his father feed a large family.

Instead of a circus, Antonio saw a redheaded missionary preaching a message that he had never heard before. He came night after night, and on January 10, 1970, he gave his heart to the Lord. His mom and dad were saved and many of his brothers and sisters. Antonio worked with us for many years before going to the United States to pastor a Spanish church.

On Sunday morning, January 17, the judge of the town was called to the tent to perform marriage ceremonies for three couples, all of whom had lived together for years without matrimony and had raised children. Then later on in the week, another man and woman were married in his office.

On January 18, the day began with a regular evangelistic service at 10:00 a.m. After this service, Christian wedding ceremonies were performed for these who had been married by the judge on Saturday. Then they came out with the food! This was a feast of cow tongue. We were the special guests, so we had plates from which to eat.

Later at the river, thirteen followed the Lord in baptism, witnessed by over two hundred people. Two men were saved by the side of the river. One was a businessman from the town.

On January 25, we held our second baptism. This time we all sang as we walked to the river. Eight were baptized. Even the judge witnessed this service!

The town of Palacagüina, a place where every known sin was practiced openly and with no standards whatsoever of morality, was greatly affected by this evangelistic campaign. Praise the Lord that He allowed us to see once again the power of the Gospel as couples were convicted of sin and had a desire to bring their lives in conformity to the Word of God.

What a precious sight to see men and women walk the aisles together—the old sawdust trail—to receive Christ.

Every missionary needs a Palacagüina experience. Only God in Heaven knows the joy we experienced in our hearts, being able to preach the Gospel to those who had never heard and to see the power of God at work. Homes were changed, and many little children now had saved mom and dads! Thank God for Palacagüina!

On the last day of the campaign, the First Baptist Church of Palacagüina was organized, and the national preacher was left as pastor. It was here that Bob knew he needed to start a Bible school to teach and train young men who were receiving Christ as their Saviour. Antonio, the fourteen-year old boy, wanted so badly to study in the Bible school, but we had very little money to run such a school. Bob also thought Antonio was too young. But a few months later at the First Baptist Church he quoted over three hundred Bible verses by memory to prove to the missionary that he was capable of learning. (He could have quoted more, but he didn't have time.) As you can imagine, Antonio came to the Bible School, and small in stature though he was, he worked alongside other men whom God was calling.

A short time ago we visited the First Baptist Church of Palacagüina. The church building was packed a 10:00 a.m. for an ordination service. Seven young preachers were ordained to the ministry. The Bible says, "Ye have not chosen me, but I have chosen you, and ordained you, that ye should go and bring forth fruit, and that your fruit should remain."

Thank God, for the souls that remained faithful in Palacagüina, Nicaragua!

10. Gospel Preached From Village To Village

"And Jesus came and spake unto them, saying, All power is given unto me in heaven and in earth. Go ye therefore, and teach all nations, baptizing them in the name of the Father, and of the Son, and of the Holy Ghost: Teaching them to observe all things whatsoever I have commanded you: and lo, I am with you always, even unto the end of the world. Amen."
—Matt 28:18-20

"Brethren, have you ever thought what one spark of fire could do in a dense forest that is as dry as a desert? This is what the Gospel can do in northern Nicaragua if this spark is placed there by the power of the Holy Spirit." Bob wrote these words in June 1970 to our supporters.

Now we can look back and see the truth and reality of that statement. More than one hundred and fifty churches and preaching stations have been raised up in Nicaragua since that day in 1970, and thousands upon thousands of people have been saved. Many were scattered during the war and are now in many places of Central America. No doubt, through their testimonies, they have won many to Christ that we won't know about until the judgment seat of Christ.

Good Samaritan Baptist Missions has over two hundred preachers and pastors, and all of these were saved in the ministry of Good Samaritan and were trained or are currently being trained and taught in the Good Samaritan Baptist Bible Institutes in Nicaragua and Honduras. In the very early days our hearts were burdened for workers. The Lord showed Bob even then the great need for a Bible Institute to teach and train national preachers so they could win their own people to the Lord. We began our first Bible Institute in the town of La Trinidad, Nicaragua, which was the second town to which we took the tent for a thirty-night campaign.

At the end of the meeting there, only twenty-five people had received the Lord out of an average of over seven hundred in attendance every night; thirteen had followed the Lord in baptism. But a harvest could not be reaped until first the seed was planted. These people had lived in spiritual darkness for centuries. The Bible was prohibited, and no one had a Bible or had ever heard the Gospel preached.

A church was organized in La Trinidad, and today this is one of the largest churches of our mission in Nicaragua. This church has started several more churches in their neighboring villages. I can remember Bob baptizing twenty-three people in one of the missions of this church—on the side of a beautiful mountain. What a blessing it was as we were able to fellowship with many of the people who had received the Lord back in May of 1970!

Before the meetings each night, I had meetings with the children, teaching them a Bible story, Bible verses and choruses. Now I am meeting pastors' wives all over Nicaragua who were in my afternoon Bible classes all those years ago. What a blessing it has been!

From the beginning these new churches were taught to be missionary-minded. In the tent meetings every night, the people stood while Matthew 28:18-20 was read. This not only verified our authority by God for being there, but it planted the seed in new Christians that they too should carry the Gospel.

Immediately they began trying to reach not only their own families and neighbors but also their neighboring villages. Many times we would walk with the congregation to a community where a lantern would be put up in a tree and a service would be held. Always there would be someone saved, and that person would open up his home for the preaching of the Gospel.

The services in the homes were a little different from the average cottage prayer meetings that Bob went to as young boy with his dad. In the homes in Nicaragua, there was hardly any furniture—maybe a chair or two and a table—so we brought our chairs with us. Someone else would bring a lantern since most of the homes had only candles. Mothers, after carrying their babies for miles, would stand for one or two hours, never complaining nor even looking tired as they listened to God's Word. Probably such poverty you have never seen, but sitting there among those Spirit-filled Christians, you would think you were among people who owned it all. Praise God, someday they will!

Our tent meetings continued in 1970 but with a larger tent and five hundred chairs that God had provided. After the chairs were completely filled, many times there would still be four and five hundred standing around the tent.

By the end of 1970, we were working in four different towns in Nicaragua. Two churches and two mission churches had been established. Seven young men were studying in the Bible institute. The church building in Palacagüina was almost completed.

How good God was to us in the early days of our missionary work, and He is still just as good, but we especially thank Him for giving us these precious memories—memories of going into villages where the people had never seen a copy of God's Word; seeing hundreds come night after night to hear His Word preached; seeing the Holy Spirit at work in the services.

We never saw great numbers saved at one time but one by one God did a work in hearts. Under heavy persecution, many, knowing they would lose their families, homes and everything they had, walked the "old sawdust trail" to receive Christ as their Saviour. Many nights we returned to our home or to a little house we had rented close to the tent, exhausted in body but so filled with the joy of the Lord that we couldn't sleep. Thank God for the memories! Our minds may be growing dim, but one day we'll remember every experience in the Lord!

11. The First Funeral

During the campaign in La Trinidad, we found a family living in an old school bus. A doctor had helped the father (Mr. Salazar) escape from a prisoner-of-war camp during the Honduras-El Salvador war many years before. The doctor found out this man had cancer and helped him get to the hospital for treatment. Mr. Salazar, along with others in his family, trusted Christ during the campaign; they were baptized and joined the church that was established after the tent campaign.

When told that Mr. Salazar was to have surgery, we wanted to be there with his wife. The surgery was scheduled at night. Bob and I were sitting in the little waiting room when the doctor came out and said, "He's gone. He died as we were trying to put him to sleep."

We were trying to console his wife, Isabel, when the door opened again, and out came the dead Mr. Salazar on a stretcher. The doctor said to Bob, "He's yours, Preacher." *Mine?* thought Bob. *What am I going to do with a dead man?* For the rest of the night, we learned what you do with a dead man.

There were no undertakers, no funeral homes, and no ambulances. The first thing needed was a casket. I stayed with Mrs. Salazar and the children—and Mr. Salazar, lying on the stretcher, mouth open, eyes open, looking straight up! —while Bob went out at midnight to try to find a casket.

A place about forty minutes away sold caskets, but Bob had a hard time waking the owner. Finally he got the casket. He remembered that Mr. Salazar would need clothes, so he went by our house and got one of his *new* suits, a tie, underwear, socks—the whole works! He got back to the hospital about 2:00 a.m. We were still there—including Mr. Salazar. By this time *I* was in a state of shock!

One of the members of the church came by about the time Bob got back, so he was there to help with dressing the corpse. They had to lift the corpse off the stretcher onto the floor, dress him, then lift him by the sheet to lay him inside the casket. Then the casket was put in our van. The church member sat on top of it. (I was taught never even to walk on a grave; now here was a man sitting on the casket!) Mrs. Salazar and the children got in, and we all went to the church.

By now it was close to daylight. Other church members came in with bouquets of flowers in tin cans, placing them around the casket. Then happened the unbelievable and unthinkable! In those days when the poor died, many times they had no clothes to put on them, so they wrapped a sheet around them and either buried them with just the sheet, or if they could obtain a wooden box, they were buried in the box. Since Mr. Salazar was poor, the ladies brought a sheet; and not paying any attention to Bob's suit, they lifted up the corpse and began wrapping the sheet around the body. "No, no, no!" exclaimed Bob. "Take that sheet off him." Bob had dressed Mr. Salazar, and he didn't want him covered in a sheet.

A service was held in the church; then we headed to the cemetery, again using our van for a hearse, while the people, carrying their little bouquets of flowers in tin cans, walked behind. Bob had paid someone to dig the grave. When we got to the cemetery, the families of Mr. Salazar, who had just arrived from El Salvador, were already there. The casket was opened again at the graveside so that they could see their loved one. They were very impressed by the way he was being "put away."

Up to this time, everything had gone pretty well. But the moment the men started putting the casket in the grave, Bob knew something was wrong! One end of the casket went in, and the other wouldn't go. And to make matters worse (and in front of all those nicely dressed Salvadoran people), some fellow got up on top of the casket and began jumping up and down, trying to make it go down in the ground!

Bob, by this time, had just about lost it. "Get off there!" he shouted. "You have to make the hole bigger."

About that time there came a cloudburst, and in the rain Mr. Salazar was buried. Thank the Lord he was saved! All that time it's possible that he may have been looking down from Heaven at all that foolishness of trying to get his body in the ground.

The doctors and others, very impressed by Bob's efforts, left an offering of over four hundred dollars—a lot of money at that time. This was for the care of Mrs. Salazar and the children. We bought her a sewing machine and materials so she could make aprons and sell them.

Sister Isabel is still with us, now in her late eighties. She still comes to church and is a blessing to everyone. She almost knows the Bible by memory—and helps the preacher out when he is looking for a Bible verse.

12. Pueblo Nuevo, Nicaragua

"So shall my word be that goeth forth out of my mouth: it shall not return unto me void, but it shall accomplish that which I please, and it shall prosper in the thing whereto I sent it."
—Isa. 55:11

January 1, 1971, found us putting up the tent in the town of Pueblo Nuevo, Nicaragua, a town that boasted, "There are no gospel believers here." God led us to hold a thirty-night tent meeting in an old western town where it was common to hear of gunfights and people being killed.

After receiving permission to put up the tent on the government plaza in the center of town, the religious leaders tried to stop us. Knowing our rights to use government property, we contacted the senator of that district, who immediately sent word back to the town leaders that we had the right to do this. We knew the reputation of this town, yet we felt a great peace and no fear.

We rented a house in the middle of town since it was too far to drive back and forth every night to our home. I got my first experience of cooking over an open fire (to feed our Bible school students). Much to our surprise, the people received us and openly showed their friendship by bringing us bananas or eggs or whatever they had.

How beautiful our new tent looked with every chair in place, the Nicaraguan and Christian flags on the platform and our Bible school students all dressed alike, many now playing musical instruments. We could not believe our eyes at the people coming—it was estimated over one thousand came every night. We had bought one hundred Bibles (a dollar each) from the capital city and were praying that there would be enough interest by the people to buy the Bibles for one dollar. (We would have gladly given them away, but we didn't have the money to do so.) We later found out that there was not *one* Bible in this whole town. People had been told all their lives that they could not understand the Bible, so they were prohibited from having a Bible because it would confuse them! By the end of the first week, every Bible had been sold. Our students went back to the capital—four hours away—to buy one hundred more. Very soon, one hundred more Bibles were sold, and we had to buy more.

The tent was filled every night. We didn't press for decisions because these people had never heard the Gospel of Jesus Christ. But what an experience to see hundreds sitting night after night listening to the gospel message!

Bob knew the Holy Spirit was dealing with a young lady under the tent, for night after night he could see conviction on her face. During the invitation she would drop her head and clench the chair in front of her. At last she walked down the aisle and received the Lord as her only Saviour.

Little did we know what was going on in her home. Her parents knew that she was interested in the Gospel, but they had threatened to send her away if she became a gospel believer. She could no longer fight the Holy Spirit, and she was saved.

Her parents were true to their promise. They sent her to the capital, saying they were getting her away from the gospel believers; but little did they know that there were many gospel believers in the capital. The Gospel had just never gone into the northern part of Nicaragua.

The second person who made a public profession of faith was an elderly lady who lived with her sister in the large temple of the village among the religious leaders. She kept the building clean. I was told that her sister hit her that night when she returned home. She never returned to the meetings.

The third person who was saved was a young man who, after the tent was taken down, rode his horse to our church in Palacagüina because there were not enough people saved in Pueblo Nuevo to start a church.

One thousand people under the tent for thirty nights and only three professions of faith! One of these was slapped, another sent away, and only one remained. It would seem like a failure, right? But God says His Word will not return void. Remember all the Bibles that were sold? God's Word was not only preached, but His Word was left among the people.

We went back to Pueblo Nuevo, Nicaragua, two more times, and on the third time a church was organized, but there were still very few believers.

What happened to the church at Pueblo Nuevo, Nicaragua? Did it ever amount to anything? This took place in 1971. Let me tell you about just some of the fruit. All happened in the years after the tent campaign.

Esteban Acuña, a young man, received the Lord in the church, but when his dad heard about it, he wouldn't let him back in the little hut. He slept outside until his grandfather showed mercy and let him come in the house. Esteban later came to our Bible school and has now been preaching for almost thirty years. He raised up some of our largest churches.

There were five Videa brothers. Ramon was the first one saved. His dad immediately ran him off but not before he led his brother Vidal to the Lord. Vidal was run off from home, but his brother Favio was saved before he left. Favio didn't wait for his father to run him off; after he received the Lord, he just put what few clothes he had in a suitcase, caught a bus and went to León, Nicaragua. His suitcase was stolen from the bus. Weeks later, one of our pastors heard about him, brought him to the Bible institute, and this was his home for many years. Another brother was baptized in secret so he could stay home but later was hung by the Sandinistas. By this time, the father's heart had softened, and Mario, the youngest was able to stay at home after he was saved.

Today, these men, all but Ramon, are missionaries. Vidal has been in Mexico for many years and has started several churches with Good Samaritan Baptist Missions. Favio raised up two churches in Costa Rica and is now pastoring a church he started in Estelí, Nicaragua. He has preached daily on Samaritan radio since its beginning. Mario is pastoring a church in Costa Rica. All four are graduates of our Bible school.

Besides the Videa brothers, there is Paulino Benavides, who was saved in Pueblo Nuevo and is now a missionary to Costa Rica.

I could go on naming the many preachers who have come out of the Pueblo Nuevo church. No church has produced as many pastors and missionaries serving with Good Samaritan Baptist Missions as the Jerusalem Baptist Church in Pueblo Nuevo, Nicaragua. The church now has its own radio station and at the last count, I was told that there were 17 missions and preaching stations.

God says we will reap if we faint not. Some plant, some water, but it is God who gives the increase.

13. Tragedy At The Bible Institute

"And we know that all things work together for good to them that love God, to them who are the called according to his purpose."—Rom. 8:28

The date was Tuesday, July 20, 1972. For over a year and a half Bob and the Bible school students had been preaching, teaching, raising up new churches and experiencing firsthand the power of God. Souls were being saved and lives were being changed.

For two days they had worked, putting the tent up in a large city called Somoto, Nicaragua. Everyone was in high spirits. One day as Bob was leaving the Bible institute to go home, he was feeling uneasy about the tent since it had begun to rain, so he asked Bayardo, one of our new and most promising students, to return to Somoto after supper to see if the tent was all right.

Later that evening we were sitting on our back porch working on programs for the meeting, which was to start the next night, when two of our students arrived. One look told us something terrible had happened. "Bayardo has killed his son," they told us. The next twenty-four hours for us were hours of horror and grief.

Alvaro, the two-year-old son of Bayardo—and a little playmate of our son—had followed his dad to the mission van as he was preparing to go check on the tent. Bayardo was completely unaware of this. Since little Alvaro was so short, Bayardo didn't see that he was standing directly in front of the van. Another student saw the whole thing, but since it happened so quickly, it was too late to stop the van. Bayardo had driven the van around the building before the screams of the student stopped him. He was unaware that he had run over and killed his only son.

One of our female students was the first to reach the little body, but his head was crushed so badly she couldn't bring herself to pick him up. Jorge, another first-year student, took the little body in his arms and started for the house. By this time the mother saw what was happening and grabbed the little body out of Jorge's arms. Now Bayardo came running around the house.

Probably five hundred people were in and around the Bible institute when we arrived. The National Guard was already there to arrest Bayardo, but the people had locked the door and were waiting for the missionaries.

We made our way through the multitude to a back room where the little body lay on the bed beside his mother and father. There were no undertakers to take the body away, prepare it and spare the family this ordeal. We talked; we prayed. What else can you do during a time like this? I thought my heart would literally burst inside me. I could not possibly imagine the agony of this mother as she lay over the child's lifeless body, moaning, "Oh, my little boy! Oh, my little creature!"

It was impossible to buy a casket that night, so we dressed him in a little suit that his dad had bought him for his second birthday two days before. We wrapped him in a sheet and laid him on a table in the large room of the Bible institute that we used for a church. The town only had a small generator for electricity, which went off at 10:00 each night; so by lantern light a service was held.

"Guilty until proven innocent" was the law of Nicaragua. Upon learning that the National Guard had come to arrest Bayardo, Bob talked to the commander and begged him not to put this grief-stricken father in jail. Finally he placed him in Bob's custody, with the promise that he would be brought in immediately after the funeral.

We returned to our home in the early hours of the morning and tried to sleep a little, but sleep does not come so easily at a time like this. I thought of our own little boy, sleeping in the next room safe and secure, and of the many times he had gone with Bob to the Bible institute where he and little Alvaro had played while Bob taught his classes.

After buying a casket for fifteen dollars and a plastic wreath of flowers, we returned to the Bible institute on Friday morning. Bayardo picked his son up off the table and put him in the casket. At 12:00 p.m. we carried the body in our van to the church in Palacagüina. It had been announced at 5:15 a.m. over our radio broadcast that Bayardo's son had died, and many people were waiting when we arrived at the church. The funeral was held at 3:00 p.m. with over three hundred in attendance.

As I watched the people bringing in the many little homemade bouquets of flowers and placing them around the casket, I thought of the deep love that was behind this. José and Miguel, two of our pastors, preached the funeral. Again the casket was put in the back of our van, and people lined up behind for the walk to the cemetery. All the little children carried flowers. The students had dug the grave that morning. Afterwards we asked Bayardo and his wife to come home with us for a few days. He was placed in Bob's custody until a complete investigation was made.

Through these investigations, Bob met Colonel Barker of our district who showed mercy on Bayardo. Through all this, he invited Bob to come to the prison of Estelí, Nicaragua, to preach to the prisoners. Only God knows the number of prisoners who were saved during the next three years as weekly services were held in the prison. Even a special room was prepared for Bob to preach and show Christian films.

All of this came about because little Alvaro lost his life. Yes, God had His purpose, and who are we to question what He does? I think of the old song "We will understand it better by and by."

14. Bob's Fight With The Demon

As my mind goes back to so many experiences that we had in the early days, I thank the Lord for allowing some of these things to happen when we were much younger!

Shortly after the First Baptist Church was built in Palacagüina, we were having a service on Wednesday night. Bob was sitting on the platform, the song leader was leading a song, and a lady was playing the accordion. All of a sudden we heard a noise at the door—everyone turned to look. A man wearing a holster and pistols rode his horse inside the church and down the aisle. He got off his horse and came to stand in front the song leader. You could see the song sheet (we didn't have hymn books) shaking in the song leader's hand. The music continued. Bob always believed in the "blood" songs and he had taught these to the people. He arose from his chair, went over to the song leader and whispered, "Sing a blood song!" The song leader quickly began singing "There is Power in the Blood," at which point the man turned around quickly and with a snarl on his face, walked back to his horse, and led him out of the church. He never uttered a word. In fact, I cannot remember anyone, not even Bob, saying anything when he left. I think we all were in a state of shock.

On one particular occasion, we were having an anniversary service in this same church. We had brought in busloads of people from our other churches. A large, closed-in truck was also filled with people who came to help us celebrate. The building was packed.

Everyone was singing. All of a sudden we heard the loud voice of a man coming down the aisle. This very big man, one of the tallest I have ever seen in Nicaragua, was shouting in Spanish. "Kill me! Kill me!" as he fell at the altar. Two deacons at once got him up and took him out the side door. The congregation kept singing. The man must have gone directly from the side door back to the front door; and back down the aisle he came, again shouting the same thing, "Kill me! Kill me!"

Bob was sitting on the platform, along with the pastor of the church. The first time this happened Bob had left it to the men of the church to handle the situation, but now he came down from the pulpit with all intentions of saying, "Mister, we love you, but we are not going to allow you to disturb this service." That's what he *intended* to say, but the man picked Bob up, held him up in the air and was carrying him out of the door before he had an opportunity to say anything.

The pastor immediately instructed the people to stay in their seats. "We have a little problem, but everything will be all right." Being the wife of the missionary, I knew if I got up and went out, others would follow. So I kept singing.

We heard running and banging. I heard someone say, "Get the knife out of his pocket!" Richard Comer, another missionary who was working with us, quickly got it before he could do any harm.

When Bob was finally able to get free, he grabbed the man and was going to throw him inside the truck, but the man grabbed Bob's tie, and both tumbled in. Bob felt the life going out of him as the man continued his "choke hold."

Finally Bob got his hands around the man's throat and squeezed until the man lost his grip. After he coughed up a large wad of phlegm, he became very calm, looked up at Bob and asked. "Am I saved now?"

The man's mother and brother came running up the road, opened his shirt and looked him over. Word had reached them that the Baptists were trying to kill him. "Your son is not hurt," Bob told the mother, "but he about killed me."

As the man started to leave, he patted Bob on the back, and these were his parting words: "God bless you, Preacher!"

This was the first and last time we ever saw him. We were told that he was a very quiet man and never bothered anyone. He was not drinking, nor was he on drugs. Until this day, we believe this was Bob's first encounter with a demon spirit—but certainly not his last!

15. A Year Of Blessings And A Year Of Suffering

1972 was a year of blessing and a year of suffering.

A campaign in Yalaguina, Nicaragua, brought twenty-eight precious souls to Christ in a town where there were no Christians. These Christians were saved under heavy persecution. Enemies to the Gospel put on white robes and with burning candles marched around the tent, shouting, "Death to the Gospel!" Can you imagine religious people doing something like that! This was the ignorance that we found in these towns and villages in northern Nicaragua when we went there. They could have easily killed us, thinking they were doing God a favor. We were accused of coming there to destroy the mother church. "We are not protesting or trying to destroy," we told them. "We will simply preach the Word of God."

What precious people God saved in Yalaguina! One of the new converts gave land adjoining his little house and store for a church. In the meantime, we brought them in by bus to our church in Palacagüina until we could build a church there. On May 28, 1972, the bus ran for the first time and in three stops picked up ninety-five people!

Also in 1972 God allowed us to buy an old rundown hotel in the town of Condega, Nicaragua, to be used for our Bible institute. We had a tent campaign here in February, and forty-seven people were saved during this campaign; twenty were baptized. The hotel had a large ballroom that would seat around four hundred, which we used for our church. Later on, we were able to build a church in the front yard of the Bible institute.

There was no electricity in this town, only a generator, operational for only a few hours a day, so the hotel had to close down. God let us buy this large building which had been used for political meetings and large festivals; then for years it became a "showplace" for the Lord. Our Bible school students lived there. They studied in the mornings, worked in the afternoons building churches, painting, cleaning or doing whatever there was to be done. At night they worked in the tent campaigns. This was our life for the next few years.

Many of our students were already pastors in the churches that had been started. What wonderful memories we have of everyone gathered on Sunday nights in the kitchen of the Bible institute to tell about God's blessings. I remember Antonio telling about a special visitor at church. "He was coming down the aisle during the invitation," Antonio said, "but he had an accident." When I asked about it, Antonio opened up the sack and dumped out a large, dead coral snake!

By the end of 1972 twelve young preachers were studying in the Bible institute. A church had been started in the village of Tranqueras, seventy miles from our mission center. It was in this church where the Lord saved Santos Casco, who later became the national director of the Nicaragua mission for many years. The Lord also saved his sister, Maura, who had an opportunity to go to Puerto Rico with Bob and other students to help in a campaign. She stayed on to help the missionary and married a young man from there. Maura has been a blessing to the church in Puerto Rico for many years, playing the accordion and helping Missionary Charles Meek in the work.

Also, a new work was started in the town of Somoto. This was where we had the tent set up when Bayardo accidentally ran over his little boy. Services were held every week in the prison, and many hardened criminals received the Lord.

Radio messages were bringing many souls to the Lord. According to reports, people were receiving Christ as they sat by their radios. This was also opening up new preaching stations.

But there were also testings and trials. When their crops died because of no rain, thousands were without food, money, or work in northern Nicaragua. One Christian lady said, "I pray that the Lord will make the stomachs of my children feel satisfied." Others had no strength to work because they were weak from not eating. With great sacrifice, we helped as many as we could. Just as Jesus took the two fishes and five loaves, brake and blessed them, He did the same with the seemingly little we had to share with others.

Little did we dream that one day He would allow us to have feeding kitchens set up in many villages to feed the hungry and clothe the naked.

"Delight thyself also in the Lord; and he shall give thee the desires of thine heart."
—*Ps. 37:4*

16. "Just Play Dead"

So many experiences God has let us remember all these years. But I am about to relate the funniest that ever happened to Bob in his mission work.

When we had an all-night meeting on Saturday night before Easter Sunday, several of our churches participated. This was held near the church in Yalaguina, underneath some large trees.

On Easter Sunday, Bob and another preacher baptized forty people, two at a time. When they had finished baptizing, Bob was very tired. Then a truck drove up. Baudilio Benavidez, a pastor from one of our very faraway missions was bringing eight new believers to be baptized! Baudilio was grinning from ear to ear, happy that he and his group had made it on time.

"Bring them on in," said Bob. He had been baptizing in an outdoor "pila," a big vat used to wash brick. Some four hundred or more were watching.

The first young lady baptized came up screaming and kicking. She had no idea what was happening to her. Bob had covered her mouth and nose as he put her *under* the water. She took his arms and pulled herself out, her face showing pure terror! This was an embarrassment to Bob. He had taught the pastors, "Instruct your people about baptism and what it is all about." These people had never seen anyone put *under* the water, and Pastor Benavidez had failed to instruct them.

The next person was a very humble-looking young man. Bob was trying to explain what he was going to do. Not knowing if the young man was understanding his Spanish, Bob said to the young man, " Just play dead. Don't try to do anything. I will put you under and bring you back up." Bob thought that was vey clear. (None of the four hundred people looking on heard any of this conversation because Bob had whispered this to the young man.)

Bob raised his hand and in Spanish started giving the formula: "In obedience to the command of our Lord Jesus Christ…" SPLOSH! He didn't finish. The boy was under the water. Bob didn't know what to do. He thought the boy had had a heart attack. Everyone, including me, was trying to get closer to see what was going on.

The young man was simply obeying what Bob had told him to do— **"play dead."** He just went into action before Bob got through with the formula. (The boy's eyes and mouth were open just like they lay out the dead in Nicaragua.) Bob said to himself, *Lord, this fellow has had a heart attack. I might as well get him out!* So he had to go all the way under, put his arms around the young man and pull him up! When his head came out of the water, the young man let out a big **"Whoopee!"** We don't think he was shouting for joy over being baptized but was shouting because Bob got him out of the water!

17. God's Mercies

The year 1973 was one of blessings, more tragedies and changes for the Tyson family in Nicaragua. On December 23, 1972, a terrible earthquake shook the capital city of Managua, Nicaragua, killing some one hundred thousand people. None of our Christians were harmed, but for months we suffered food and water shortages.

In March 1973 of necessity our family moved into the Bible institute building, the old hotel building we had recently purchased. Young men and women were living there studying the Bible, and we needed to be there to supervise them.

It was not easy. Managua was completely destroyed by the earthquake, so food was limited. We didn't mind eating beans and rice, but not for every meal. We had no refrigeration other than an ice chest, and the ice had to come from twenty-five miles away. We quickly became accustomed to drinking powdered milk.

Another adjustment facing us was the lack of electricity. The weak electrical system operated from 7:00 p.m. until 10:00 p.m.; then everything was completely dark. Bob admitted looking at poles and power line and beginning to covet. He could see the beauty in the power lines running through other towns! But he reminded me of that day when he had promised the Lord that he would go **anywhere** and do **anything** He wanted him to do.

When one asked him how he ever found his way to the bathroom at night, his answer was: "Waiting on a car to come down the Pan American

Highway with its headlights on. I took advantage of this to get to the bathroom real fast. To get back to the bedroom I had to wait for another car to come by."

On July 17, 1973, amidst all these conditions, our second son, Stevie, was born. There were many complications, but thank the Lord for a good doctor who had recently moved to Estelí, having lost everything in the earthquake in Managua. Stevie was born prematurely, and living in an area with no electricity or other conveniences made caring for him hard. Oh, God was with us in those days!

The doctor told us that Stevie was in bad shape and needed to be put in an incubator. "We have one," he said, "but it won't work." Bob began tinkering with it, and soon it was working. Stevie's color was blue, and he was cold. When put in the incubator, his color came back, and he got warm. When we saw him turn blue again, we just turned up the oxygen. However, later in the United States, in a book on premature babies, I read: "The reason for blindness in many premature babies is that they were given too much oxygen in the incubator." We thought we were helping Stevie, yet we could have caused blindness. How good and merciful God is!

Stevie is such a blessing to the work. He is married to a beautiful Honduran girl named Scarleth. Stevie is director of the Samaritan Radio Network and works in the administration of the mission in San Marcos de Colón. He and Scarleth have two beautiful little girls, Ashley and Brianna.

One year earlier, in 1972, after much prayer and seeking God's will, we left the mission board we were with and became completely independent. We simply wrote our supporters and told them we wanted to represent them directly. For a long time this had been on our hearts. We never left the field. We simply wrote a letter to the churches that supported us. Bob's burden was to win souls and train and help support the national preachers. He felt he had to work as God led him. We told our supporters if they felt led to continue our support, to send it directly to Nicaragua. Our support doubled in just a short time, proving to us once again that God was our Great Provider.

In October 1973 it was necessary for us to return to the United States and charter Good Samaritan Baptist Missions, Inc. God had blessed in such a way that, had we not chartered a nonprofit organization, we would have been personally responsible for a lot of money and taxes. The name *Good Samaritan* came from our ministry in Sherwood, Tennessee. Our good friend and lawyer, L.S. Cobb, did all the work free of charge.

By the end of 1973, we were in the process of building a new kitchen and dormitories at the Bible institute. The new church building in Yalaguina could not hold all the people. A member of the church in Pueblo Nuevo had given land for a building there.

Over a thousand were in Sunday school every Sunday. Our burden in 1973—which has not changed today—was to see Nicaragua saturated with the Gospel. How important it is that every person has an opportunity to hear how to be saved. And how important that every Sunday school teacher present the Gospel in a simple way to precious boys and girls.

I recall one Sunday at 3:00 p.m. when a little nine-year-old girl was struck by a jeep and killed instantly. She had ridden the bus to Sunday school that morning. I asked the Sunday school teacher that day, "Maura, did you realize this morning when you were teaching that one of your pupils might go out into eternity in just a few hours? Are you sure you made the plan of salvation simple enough so that she could know how to be saved?"

What an important task God had given us! We still have that task today.

18. "And That Your Fruit Should Remain"

Two other missionary families worked with us in the early seventies—Richard and Patty Comer and Darrel and Shirley Dean. Both couples were a blessing to us and to the work. Richard taught in the Bible institute and helped in the tent meetings and churches. Darrell was the kind of missionary who could do about anything, could help in any needed area, especially with the buses. Every bus could be running perfectly, but on Sunday morning, one or two would fail to start. The Devil has always hated the bus ministry.

March 1974 we entered the small town of Totogalpa. It could never again be said that there were no Christians in this place. Eighteen adults and young people were saved in these meetings. Thirty rode the bus every Sunday to the church in Yalaguina. Years later, when the communists took over Nicaragua, we were able to visit this little church in Totogalpa. I saw a young man, his wife and baby standing next to the church. When I went over to introduce myself, the young mother said, "Why, Sister Joan, you know me! You taught me in Sunday school when I was a little girl in the church of Yalaguina." Now this young lady was the pastor's wife in Totogalpa. Can you imagine how those words made me feel? "...And that your fruit should remain" (John 15:16).

How many times the Devil falsely accused us, saying our work had been in vain. But God gives us these moments and experiences to show us that **our work for God has never been and will never be in vain.**

19. Without Shame

"For I am not ashamed of the gospel." —Rom. 1:16

In April 1974 we began a thirty-night meeting in the large city of Estelí, Nicaragua. The tent was filled every night. Some sixty people made professions of faith in Christ. At the end of the meeting, twenty-nine followed the Lord in beautiful believer's baptism in a nearby river.

Always there were comical things happening to us. As I have said, a missionary must learn to laugh at himself. Bob was completely overjoyed at the response to the invitation during these services. Most of the time we would see only a few saved; but in Esteli, the Holy Spirit worked, and the people filled the altar night after night. One night after eighteen precious people had come forward and were gloriously saved, he had them line up in front to give their testimonies. With the microphone in hand, he went down the line to hear each tell what Jesus had done for him.

Remember, in Spanish you can get just one letter or one phrase wrong or said in a different way, and it **completely** changes the whole context of what you want to say. This is what he wanted to say or what he thought he said to that audience of over five hundred people that night after the testimonies were given: "Here are eighteen brave, courageous people who are not ashamed to testify of the saving grace of Jesus Christ." But that is **not** what came out in Spanish. This is what he actually said: "Here stand eighteen of the sorriest, low-down, good-for-nothing people who would stab their own grandmas in the back."

He had used the words *sin verguenza*, which means "without shame." He wanted to say they were not ashamed but had used it in the wrong way.

Needless to say, people were falling out of their chairs in laughter! Bob stood there, wondering what in the world he had said wrong. I too was in the dark. Seated by Patty Comer, I asked, "Patty, what did he say?" But she was laughing so hard she couldn't even answer me!

No one was offended because they all knew what he meant.

Such fun we have remembering the struggle Bob had with that language and some of the mistakes he made! **Love** covers a multitude of sins, thank the Lord!

A Missionary Journey

20. Teaching Faithful Men

Years ago we were awakened at 5:00 a.m., by a noise outside our living room window. Looking out the window, Bob saw thousands marching behind idols and chanting "prayers." Some were even walking on their knees, literally shedding their own blood, trying to gain favor and forgiveness from idols that could neither see nor hear. "O God," cried Bob, "what can one man do to reach the multitudes living in complete darkness?" He said that a small voice whispered to him, "One man can´t but an army can".

"And the things that thou hast heard of me among many witnesses, the same commit thou to faithful men, who shall be able to teach others also." —*II Tim. 2:2*

And so it has been down through the years—faithful men teaching faithful men.

In August 1974 we held our first Bible school graduation. Three pastors and a pastor´s wife were the first to graduate after three and one-half years of studying the same material that we had received at Tennessee Temple University.

God gave the answer in the above Scripture verse, and for many years, this is what Bob tried to do. God has raised up a small army of national preachers. All have been saved in the ministry of Good Samaritan, and all have studied or are currently studying in the Good Samaritan Bible Institute. There are graduations and ordinations every year, sending young men out to preach the Word of God. The ministry has grown, not because of Bob or Joan Tyson but because of faithful men teaching faithful men. And it never stops. God has the perfect plan.

21. El Coral

When Christians moved to a new town or village, their first concern was a church where they could worship. Such was the case of the Tercero family who moved way back into the mountains of New Guinea into a community called El Coral, named for the coral snake.

We were all excited as we loaded up two vans with equipment for an evangelistic meeting in New Guinea. Bob, Philip, Stevie, and I, along with a big group of students, headed out for the ten-hour trip, which was mostly on dirt roads. It was a day's journey and almost dark when we pulled into the yard of a small church that the Tercero family had built with their own money. All they needed now were people to fill it up; so they called us.

That first night all of us were so hungry after eating only snacks on the journey (there were no fast-food restaurants along the way). A table was prepared outside for students; and Bob, the boys, and I were served chicken stew inside the Tercero's little store. There was only a lantern for light, but the food was good. Bob always said I go overboard bragging on anything served to us but it is because I want people to know how much we appreciate their sacrifice. I guess I went overboard again because they were so proud that we liked the chicken stew, it was served to us at every meal! How I envied our students, who were fed beans, rice, tortillas, and cheese. Many times I would sneak out there to finish my meal with them!

In the daytime, we could see where and what we were eating. The hogs and chickens walked around for some crumbs. One night I couldn't get my feet under the table because the hog went to bed early!

The girls slept on coffee sacks and bean sacks in the store, and the boys slept in the church. Our family slept in the back of our van parked underneath some trees. When I heard that the place was named for the coral snake and we were parked under some trees, my imagination went wild. The snakes could fall out of the trees and come in through the open window; so it was "roll up the windows" or move the van. It was very hot, but we decided to roll up the windows.

I was also content to go to the river and bathe until I heard about the snakes. For the rest of the time we were there, I bathed in a little wooden bathhouse. This simply means you have a place to get in (no roof) to pour a bucket of water over your head. Stevie also was afraid of snakes, so I bathed him in the bathhouse. When I pulled off his shoes, he got a fungus from the wet floor, and for weeks the skin literally fell off his little feet.

I was home-schooling Philip, but there was no way I could keep his attention off the monkeys running up and down the trees. I finally decided that living in the jungles for a week was an education in itself.

In the store where we ate, a giant lizard was tied up, and I had to pass it if I had any plans to sneak food from the students. They kidded me all week that they were going to feed me lizard, which was good for your brain. They did kill the lizard our last night there; and Mr. Tercero, the eighty-year-old head of the clan, and José, one of our preachers, had a lizard feast. I had watched Mr. Tercero as he bought and sold beans and coffee, and he didn't even use an adding machine! He had a sharp mind, so maybe lizard was good for the brain, but I never felt led to eat any of it!

The meetings started. The first night the little church was about three-fourths full. The next night the benches had to be moved out into the yard. Every night the attendance grew. People began to trust the Lord and get saved. Some people would walk for hours to get to the meeting, and after the service, they would lie down on the ground for a few hours' sleep. We could hear them stirring around between three or four o'clock in the morning, leaving for a long walk back up the mountain where they worked in the fields all day before coming back for services the next night.

We were strangers, sleeping in a van while others slept on the ground all around us. No houses, just a store building with a little church beside it—but a peace we can't explain hovered over that place.

There were a lot of tears when we said good-bye. We never went back, but a church was left with saved people. A national preacher moved there, and today this church has grown to seven more churches and missions!

Chicken stew, lizard, snakes, bathing in the river and bathhouses—unforgettable memories! But the one thing I remember most is lying on the floor of that van night after night, with so many people lying on the ground around us, and feeling God's presence and perfect peace.

22. "Who Shall Separate Us From The Love Of Christ?"

As missionaries working in areas where there were no doctors or medical help for miles, there were always times of sadness along with the blessings. These were opportunities for us to minister not only spiritually but also physically. Many times we felt heartbroken as we saw the suffering of people we had come to love as our own families.

An outside oven filled with hot coals had been cleaned, and while playing, the two-year-old daughter of one of the members in the church of Tranqueras ran into these hot coals. Her mother heard her screams. These people lived seventy-five miles from any doctor, and as it was Holy Week, not even a bus was running. Their only hope was the missionaries who were coming the next day for services. Can you imagine the suffering this child went through for over twenty-four hours?

When we entered the village and found what had happened, we didn't conduct a service but immediately put the little girl in our van and began the long trip back to the town of Estelí. She had cried so much that now she could only moan. She lay on the seat of the van with her little feet in my lap. Every time the van hit a bump on the dirt road, the little girl would show the excruciating pain.

We reached Estelí hospital that night. She was there for seventeen days, but she didn't lose her feet. Praise God! Today, thirty-four years later, this little girl is now a wife and mother.

* * *

On one occasion, a young mother came running to our Bible institute with her baby gasping for breath and laid the little one in my arms. There was no doctor in this town, and the mother's only hope was to try to get her baby to the missionary. She believed we were sent by God and could save her. Can you imagine the turmoil I felt looking into the faces of a dying child and a mother who was expecting a miracle! What could I do? For the first time in our lives as missionaries, we had a car with air conditioning. I called a Bible school student to go with me, put the baby's face against the air-conditioner vent and set out on the twenty-five mile journey to the doctor. The baby was still alive when we reached the doctor, and her little life was saved.

* * *

"Who shall separate us from the love of Christ? shall…famine?" —Rom. 8:35

We saw Nicaragua go through a great drought, and there was a great famine in the land. We realized just how critical things were when hundreds came to the government grain bins to buy corn for tortillas and were turned away. There was just no more corn to be sold. Many lived by eating tortillas made of cornmeal.

One of our deacons asked what we would do if the Christians began dying of starvation. The Bible says that we are tested by fiery trials, and certainly this was a test of our Good Samaritan spirit as we worked among thousands of hungry people. It is saddening to live day-by-day seeing unbelievable poverty, suffering and a sense of hopelessness. Could we say, 'Go ye and be filled' (Jas. 2:16)?

Along with the hungry stomachs, we saw a hunger for the Word of God. Our task was harder as we tried to minister to suffering people. But God always provided. On one occasion we sent food for the church of Tranqueras. When news reached us that these Christians had divided their portions with their neighbors, Bob was so upset. He questioned, "O God, how can we feed a whole country?" We had only sent enough for the church people.

The next time we visited the church in Tranqueras, I was amazed to see so many people, especially adults. One by one these strangers stood, giving their testimonies of how these church members had shared their food with them when they really needed it themselves. "It showed us what real Christianity is all about." Because of this, many were saved. We had more men in the church of Tranqueras than in any other church.

23. Light Of The Jungle

The year of 1975 was another year of hard work but many blessings. Six campaigns, each of thirty nights, resulted in 244 professions of faith and 115 baptisms. One hundred seven were saved in the tent meeting, and a church was established in the large city of Ocotal, Nicaragua.

One Friday afternoon a man came walking up to the mission center in Condega. He asked for our national preacher, José Santos Espinoza, who preached daily on the radio. Bob told him that José was preaching a few miles away and if he wanted to go, he would take him to the service.

That night this man went forward to give a testimony. He told of listening to the Gospel over his little battery radio back in the jungles of Wiwili, Nicaragua. The radio preacher asked if anyone wanted to be saved. If so, he should kneel wherever he was, repent and ask the Lord to save him. He said he did this in the middle of his bean patch where he was working.

Immediately, he said, there came a desire to tell that radio preacher that he had received the Lord. So he made plans to come to Condega. He had to walk for eight hours out of the jungles, walk for several more miles, and take a raft down the river, then a bus to Condega.

He stayed with us until Sunday, was baptized in a large vat in front of our Bible institute, and then made his way back to the jungle. Several months later, word reached us that over fifty people had been saved; now he needed some one to come and baptized them. A group of our national preachers went and baptized fifty-seven people. Not many months went by before the national preachers were called again to baptize forty more. Every household but one had been saved. This "jungle brother" had given land, and a church had been built. The building materials had to be tied on donkeys to make the journey back into the jungles.

He never became a preacher, but he taught Sunday school in the church that they named Light of the Jungle Baptist Church. His desire was to see his whole village come to know the Lord as he knew Him.

One day after Sunday school, two men of the church were on the porch of the church talking. They saw this brother going across the field toward his little house. Then they saw him fall on his knees. These two commented that he was praying there in the middle of his field. Then suddenly he went forward falling on his face, dead.

He had finished his work; he had won the race; he had finished his course; now there was waiting for him a crown of righteousness. And not for him alone, but for all of us who are faithful, who finish our course.

Later, it was our great privilege to meet Brother Luis Lopez. He was saved in the Light of the Jungle Baptist Church and has been pastor there for many years. Brother Luis was faithful throughout the many war years. He had bean beaten almost to death on two occasions by the communists, his sixteen-year-old boy was killed because he refused to fight for communism, and the church building was burned. But Brother Luis remained faithful—now old and his face drawn from the suffering and pain—but **faithful.**

Bob looked at Luis's skinny arms, pulled off his own watch and put it on Luis's wrist. It dangled on his arm, but he was so appreciative.

During the war in Nicaragua the church building was burned and the people had been meeting in a house. A few years ago, God laid it on the heart of our good friend, Paul Shepard, to build them a new church. The only problem—when the church was finished, Bro. Paul wanted to go and see it. I say a problem because Bro. Paul was almost 80 years old and Light of the Jungle is on top of a very, very high mountain with no travelable road reaching this area. I tried to discourage him every way I could. One of our pastors in Nicaragua even took a video camera and filmed as he journeyed by foot up the trail to the church, which took several hours. As he was filming, a snake that was wrapped around a tree, stuck his head out and hissed at him. I thought surely this would discourage Bro. Paul, but after seeing the video, his first words were, "Should we take sleeping bags?"

Well, I could see then that Bro. Paul had made up his mind. So I begged the pastors to please take good care of him. I don't know how many pastors went with him but he arrived safely at the church in Light of the Jungle. I believe some of the trip was made on a mule or donkey and the pastors were all there to help for any emergency. Only the pastor and a few were there when he arrived but in just a few minutes, he said there were people coming from everywhere.

Thank the Lord for the radio; thank the Lord for the first man saved who became a missionary and won almost all his village to the Lord, and thank the Lord for Bro. Paul Shepard who not only gave but who had the courage to go.

24. Sleeping With The Spiders

In March 1978 when a large group visited us from the U.S., we thought it would be nice to take them to one of our new works located in Wiwili, Nicaragua. Eighty-six people had been baptized there in about six months, and there were more waiting to be baptized. Bob had made the trip once, finishing the last leg of his journey in a canoe.

We left the mission center at 8:00 a.m., traveling over dirt roads in a diesel bus until 3:30 p.m. We then transferred to large four-wheel-drive trucks in order to cross the river, then traveled by narrow roads for forty-five more minutes. About one hundred fifty people were waiting for us—some had been waiting all day, anxious to see, for the first time, people from the United States. We went immediately to the river where six of the visiting pastors participated in a beautiful baptismal service.

Turkeys were being stewed in large vats. I had brought bread and coffee (their homegrown coffee would be much too strong for Americans). The pastor had assured us when we made plans for the trip that there would be a place for everyone to sleep. I was concerned about clean sheets for the beds, unaware that sheets should have been the least of my worries!

After supper, the service started outside. There was only a lantern for light, but a multitude was in attendance. And we were all chilled before the service ended.

Bob came to me with that look that I don't like to see. "We have problems," he said. "One of the men, Brother Harold Howard, wants to check into his room."

"What about the motel?" I whispered. (I cannot imagine why we would think there was a motel back in those jungles.)

"I've been down the hill," Bob said. "There's no motel—just some cow stalls."

As I looked around at Brother Randy Hardeman, pastor of Glen Haven Baptist Church in Atlanta, I remembered Brother Ralph Easterwood, the co-pastor, saying, "Brother Randy is not well. You all take real good care of him." I looked at Brother John Everhart, pastor of Wrenn Memorial Baptist Church, Greenville, South Carolina, and a faithful supporter for years and years. Brother Doug Tate, a pastor in Alabama, was on his first mission trip. And there were Brother William Thompson and many others— —all cold, tired and waiting to "check in." Brother Harold Howard was also still waiting to "check in."

"O God, help me not to panic," I prayed.

You might ask, "Why did the pastor not tell you there was no place to sleep?" I asked him the same question a few minutes later. To tell the truth, he was so excited at the thoughts of having all these North Americans visit his church that he didn't exactly lie—nor exactly tell the truth. There were places to sleep—but for animals, not for a group of visitors from the United States!

Fernando pointed to the only house in sight and said there were one bed and two cots in there. There were two or three canvas one-person cots in the "cow stalls." Fortunately, we had brought two or three cots on the bus— just in case they were needed at the "motel!"

Bob took the lantern and led the way to the stalls. All the pastors meekly followed behind. Being the "humble" pastors that they were, no one said a word or showed any emotion in front of Bob. They chose their own sleeping partners, and Bob took the lantern and left.

Meanwhile, the rest of us were waiting to get "checked in." I felt sort of bad that we were getting the house while the others were getting cow stalls down the hill. But a few minutes later, I would have gladly traded.

The house had one double bed and two canvas cots. We decided to put Brother Dan Howard, his wife, his mother-in-law and the missionary Patty Comer crossways on the bed. (Someone from Alabama had sent us fifty dollars and told us to use that to treat Brother Dan *really well* because he could *really* help the work in Nicaragua.) Brother Champ and Dianne Agan, Bob, and I got the two cots.

Brother Dan got the lantern and was looking around when he discovered–not one, not two, but—**walls** matted with grayish-white tarantula spiders! We're talking about hundreds! "We can't stay here!" he shouted. Bob knew he was about to panic, so he grabbed the lantern and said, "You're going to cause everyone to panic. Give me that lantern and go to bed!"

Well, so much for the fifty dollars and taking care of Brother Dan!

With fear and trembling (and the windows filled with the faces of people looking in at these strange Americans), we lay down for the night, with the lantern burning. All of a sudden, the pastor's voice came through the window: "Brother Bob, the people walked a long way, and they want to have services all night."

"No problem," replied Bob. "You all go ahead, but we're real tired."

To which the pastor replied, "But you have our only lantern."

So we gave up our lantern, put our cots in the middle of the floor just in case one or more of the spiders decided to turn loose and fall.

Meanwhile, down at the cow stalls Brother John and Brother Randy were huddled together on their little cot in their private stall. All of a sudden they heard roosters crowing. Brother Randy commented, "Praise God, John! We've made it!" They looked at a watch and it was just 11:30! (Roosters in Nicaragua crow at all times during the night.)

Lying there in the darkness and with spiders all around us, we had a peace from God that passeth all understanding. How could we be afraid as we listened to people singing the old hymns that Fernando had taught them—"At the Cross," "There is Power in the Blood," "There is a Fountain Filled With Blood," "Amazing Grace"—their voices ringing out through the jungle.

I will never forget the next morning when Brother Harold Howard came to me with his little china cup that he took everywhere he went and humbly asked, "Sister Joan, do you think I could get some coffee?"

"Sure, Brother Harold. I brought some instant with me, and I'll find some water."

A large black pot was boiling over an open fire on the ground, so I asked the woman if we could have some water for coffee. "Yes, of course," she answered in Spanish. To our astonishment, she simply tipped the black pot over, held back all the eggs that were boiling and filled Brother Harold's little china cup. He looked as if he were going to cry.

"Sister Joan, I don't believe I can drink that to save my life." About that time Bob walked up and, seeing what was going on, said, "Bless God! Give it to me. I can!"

Meanwhile, Sister Dianne Agan, with never a hair out of place and as neat as a pin, called out, "Bother Bob, do you think there is anywhere I could plug in my hair dryer?"

"Not unless you brought a 100-mile drop cord," Bob answered.

As we loaded on the backs of those trucks that morning, we all looked like we had been to a cantina all night instead of a church service. But, my, the peace and joy in our hearts! Just to know that there are people back in the jungles who love Jesus, who are saved and who, one day, will have mansions in Heaven.

We waved good-bye to all the people and the national preacher, who counted it a privilege to live in El Carmen, Wiwili, and preach to them the Gospel.

Thank God for these memories of Wiwili, Nicaragua!

25. God's Protection

We had lived in the mission center for several years; but needing someone to help us in the work so badly, we gave our rooms in the center to a new missionary family and moved to our Terry camper out in the backyard.

We had no meetings this particular night, so we read to the boys and put them to bed over the kitchen table. Our bedroom consisted of two half beds, with a cabinet on each side of the beds and a back bathroom. Bob and I ate some watermelon, and then we went to bed.

Around 2:00 a.m. I was lying with my face to the little window, sound asleep, when I felt something cold and wet touch my back. I whirled over immediately. "Something" fell to the floor. In my imagination, it was a dog. I tried to wake Bob, who was lying just on the other side. I didn't scream because I thought, *This has to be the bravest Nicaraguan dog I have ever seen, and if I scream, he will attack me.* He kept lying on the floor. I could see only a little by the dim light out in the backyard (we now had electricity at the mission center).

I continued trying to wake Bob with a low voice, but to no avail. I then started trying to back up on the little bed so I could get to the bathroom without stepping on the "dog." As I began to back up, the "dog" ran out the door. As soon as I heard his feet hit the steps, I called out in a loud voice. This woke Bob.

"What's the matter?" he asked.

"There's been a dog in here," I answered.

"A dog! How in the world could a dog get in the trailer?"

"I don't know," I said, "but there was a dog in here."

I got out of bed, and sure enough, I saw the door was half open. Without much light to see, I merely closed the door and went back to bed.

The longer I lay there, the more upset I became with Bob.

Finally he said, "I don't know why you are so upset with me; I didn't leave the door open."

I thought for a moment, then said, "When you threw the watermelon rind out, you left it open."

To this Bob quickly replied, "I never threw the watermelon rind out. I put it in the trash."

Uh-oh! He hadn't opened the door again, and I *knew* I had locked it before going to bed.

Up I got, and this time I turned on the light. A large round hole had been cut in the middle of our door! Papers, receipts, etc., were scattered all over the yard. Undoubtedly, someone was looking for money. We were building two church buildings, and we kept money in the cabinet above my bed. We had no bank in our town, but a "rolling bank" came twice a week and cashed our checks. I still had the checks that had not been cashed, because the day before had been a holiday and the "bank" hadn't come. Whoever came into the trailer must have known where to go, for he took the two money boxes—one for each construction—and went outside. When he didn't find much money, he came back in and began searching me. (Many Nicaraguan women carry money pinned underneath their clothes.)

Upon checking, we found a watch had also been stolen and the heart gone out of the watermelon we had put in the refrigerator. This accounted for the wet, cold hand that was touching my body.

A member of the National Guard came immediately, and here were his words to Bob: "You had better thank your God that your wife didn't scream, because with the same machete that was used to cut open the door, you both would have been killed." He went on to explain that just one person did not do this. "They work in pairs, and they take off their shirts so they can't be seen easily." It was the same pattern the rebels were using to steal and kill, financing the war that was about to begin.

Why was it so hard to awaken Bob when he is a light sleeper? The guard also told us that in these robberies, gas is sprayed through the window to put the victim or victims in a deep sleep. We knew that it was God who protected us.

We are not immune from bad things happening in this world, but God is in control, and Satan has no power to take lives without His permission. For this reason, we can work and live in dangerous places with the complete peace and faith in our Heavenly Father.

26. Stranded In Mexico

In 1977 the seemingly impossible happened. Civil war broke out in Nicaragua. Although we thought the strong Somoza army would never be brought down, the Sandinistas took over Nicaragua in 1979.

Sporadic fighting had been going on all over northern Nicaragua for several months, especially back in the mountains. Even when we made our trip with the group to Wiwili, we saw armed men behind sandbags and in trenches; but as long as God gave us peace, we would never think of leaving our work there.

Sunday, March 5, 1977, at 2:30 a.m., our beautiful little church in front of the mission center was burned to the ground. We understand now how persecution only makes the Christian stronger. One of the members said, "The Gospel of Jesus Christ must not be stopped. We will meet under the trees. Our building may be burned, but they will never burn the real church—those of us who are washed by the blood of Jesus Christ."

Our future as resident missionaries became very uncertain. We knew, however, that this would not affect the churches, because for ten years the ministry had been built around the nationals. It was not easy to preach with demonstrations, rioting, killings and burning all around; however, the national preachers continued to preach and see souls saved.

Many of our people, especially our pastors, became very concerned for our safety. In September 1977, we decided to go to the United States for a short leave until things "cooled down." Little did we realize on that

Tuesday afternoon as our many friends and national workers gathered around us and prayed for our safety, that we would encounter many ordeals and go through trials *before* reaching the United States.

In El Salvador our water pump burst. When we pulled in at a trailer park in Guatemala, Bob was so sick that a man in the park had to park the car and trailer. Bob had one chill after another. We were there for two days. What caused his illness, we never knew. And we had no idea what was ahead for us.

Our car almost burned up twice in Mexico, and we were stranded time and time again. We were pulling a travel trailer, and our car and trailer were too wide to pull off the road, blocking big tractor-trailer trucks coming from both directions. Many times the boys and I would sit up on the bank or out in the field in the hot sun, waiting for Bob, who was trying to find water to get the car going again. We were in a desert—no houses, no telephones. We did have a little food and a little water in the trailer.

When we finally were able to get news back to the States that we were stranded in Mexico, Max Furr, now with the Lord, immediately went to work to get someone to help us. He personally gave a thousand dollars to have the car repaired. And Missionary Richard Comer flew in from Tampa, Florida. When Richard arrived, he said, "I'll stay and help, but Joan and the boys need to get out of here."

At 4:00 in the morning Bob went with us by taxi to an airstrip about two hours away to catch a small plane flying to Mexico City. I cried all the way. I was leaving Bob sick; a war was going on in Nicaragua; and we didn't know what was happening to the Christians, the churches and our mission families. It almost seemed all over for us, and what an awful feeling!

Bob and Richard worked on the car in temperatures of 110 degrees and above. Again and again the car would go a few miles, then get so hot it couldn't possible go further. Parts for the motor had to be brought in twice from the United States.

On a Sunday morning they had a service—just the two of them. Bob picked the guitar, and both sang and testified. They hugged each other, and they cried. After twenty-one days on the road, two very tired and rather thin missionaries arrived home. A book could be written about those twenty-one days stranded in Mexico.

27. House In Georgia

Through the help of Pastor Champ Agan and his wife, Dianne, we settled in a house they had rented for us near their home in Hiram, Georgia. In just a few weeks this house was sold, and we were house-hunting again.

The real estate agent took us to a house in Villa Rica that was for sale or for rent. As we got out of his car, we recognized the man who was painting inside the carport—our old friend, Pastor Wendell Rush. Immediately, Brother Rush wanted to sell us the house. (A builder had built two houses side by side; then when God called the builder to be a missionary in Guatemala, he rented one of the houses to a preacher, and Brother Wendell bought the other—just to help the missionary be able to get on the field.)

"Brother Wendell, we don't even have any credit. We haven't bought anything on credit for over fifteen years," Bob told him. Brother Wendell, almost begging us to buy the house, said, "Just take up the notes, and it would be less money than paying rent."

When I told him we didn't have a stove or refrigerator, he said he would put them in for us. He would also go to the bank with Bob…and on and on.

It would be nice, we admitted, to have a home to come to when we came back to the States, instead of living out of suitcases. But we had never even thought about buying a house since going to the mission field. Little did we know that all of this was in God's future plans for us and that He was using Brother Wendell Rush to bring this about.

Should we ever doubt God and His leading? He goes before us, plans it all out, and has people there for us.

Let me tell you the rest of the story.

Bob went to the bank with Brother Wendell and with no trouble got a loan. In fact, our payments would be only $188.00 a month. We were then paying $248.00 for rent.

We bought the house, moved in, and then closed it back up immediately to return to Honduras to await the fate of our beloved Nicaragua.

Upon our return to the States several months later, a gentleman knocked at our back door. He talked to us about the two empty lots behind our house. His wife needed surgery, and he had to sell them, "and since they are so close to your house, I want you to have the first opportunity." He needed a few hundred dollars down, and we would take up small payments—just sixteen dollars a month on one and twenty-eight on the other.

We bought them only for security reasons (we thought)—to keep someone from building in our backyard.

After the war ended in Nicaragua and we were sending in needed food and clothing, we desperately needed a place to store these things. God's plan was coming into force. Another good friend, R. J. Reese, who owned a construction company, agreed to build a storage building for us on one of the empty lots. Brother R. J. put his men to work, not charging one cent. Others came in and helped. R. J. asked if I would mind if he put in some windows and kitchen cabinets. He would pay for them. He said, "Only the Lord knows what this building will be one day." I said, "Brother R. J., do whatever you want to do." Another pastor, William Thompson, furnished the wallpaper and paint.

While Bob and I visited churches, these friends and pastors worked. When they finished, we had a pretty four-room house. Today it is the office of Good Samaritan Baptist Missions. God had it all planned out.

On the second lot, we have a double-wide for missionaries and others to use.

God put us through a time of transition. He was making plans, then carrying them out. What He would lead us to do in the future was beyond all our imaginations.

28. Mission Center Taken Over By Sandinistas

Since so much happened in 1979, it's hard to write this chapter.

We closed up the house we had bought in Vila Rica, Georgia and headed once again to Nicaragua. Plans were made to stay for one month in Merida, Mexico, and help missionaries Richard and Patty Comer. We had invited several of our preachers from Nicaragua to help us in this evangelistic campaign. Thank the Lord, they had no problem leaving the country.

Many were saved in the meetings in Mexico; and in May 1979, we headed out once again, hoping to go into Nicaragua. By the time we arrived in Honduras, the situation had grown more critical. It was impossible for us to go into Nicaragua. Our beautiful mission center had been taken over by five hundred Sandinista soldiers—the place where so many of our national preachers had lived and studied God's Word. This, which had been their home and ours for years, was now the military headquarters for the Sandinistas for the entire North. It included a courtroom, a jail, and even the tomb of the unknown soldier was in the front yard. President Somoza sent in warplanes to bomb these rebels out. Everyone told us that the building would be completely destroyed, but once again God intervened. This was His property, and He still had a purpose for this mission center. Not one windowpane was broken!

Much to everyone's surprise, the Sandinistas mounted machine guns on the upstairs balcony and shot down two of Somoza warplanes. They took one of the fallen planes out of the river and pulled it up to the side of a hill. Today it is still mounted, showing the power of the Sandinistas.

About a year earlier, we had bought our very first piano from a missionary who was leaving the field. With great sacrifice, we paid a thousand dollars for it. A little thing, but it shows that God uses small things to teach us great lessons. I just knew the piano would be destroyed—but it wasn't. The story goes that when one of the soldiers came in from battle, he played the piano. When he left, he locked it because he didn't want anyone "banging" on it.

Many pastors had put their lives on the line, standing up to Sandinista officers, trying to convince them that moving into the mission was wrong. The first commander, when told that this property belonged to God, proudly boasted, "Here the government comes first, and God comes second." A few days later this commander, while driving through the mountains, lost control of his jeep and went off a high cliff. The jeep was loaded with explosives, and his body was blown into many little pieces. The second officer in charge said they had nowhere else to go, that this was the largest and most ideal place for their headquarters.

It seemed an impossible situation then, but our people never gave up. **God works in mysterious ways.**

One of our church members, Mrs. Petrona, went through a terrible experience during the war. Huddled in her bedroom with her two little boys, she and her children listened as the entire family on the other side of the wall was being brutally murdered—the children's throats were slashed as their mother screamed in terror. Everyone blamed this on the government soldiers, and this was a major turning point for Mrs. Petrona.

For a time she was in a state of shock, then hospitalized. Afterwards, she became sympathetic towards the Sandinistas. At their victory, she was given a job in one of their offices. She came to know a lot of the Sandinista officials, so she went from office to office, using all her influence to get our mission property back.

One day the seemingly impossible happened. Large trucks and vans backed up to the mission center. All the machine guns, the weaponry, jeeps, tanks—everything pertaining to war—was hauled out. Even the unknown soldier was dug up. Then God's property was given back to our preachers.

The Lord showed His power. Only through Him could we have gotten this property back. After one year, the soldiers and their operation moved out, and the property was returned to Good Samaritan Baptist Missions—and the piano was still intact.

It was later used once again in His work. We couldn't say that for the kitchen cabinets which were used for firewood in the backyard. They didn't use the kitchen stove. The walls were smeared with blood from the wounded soldiers. I feel sure many died in this building.

The day our charter with the Nicaraguan government was to be approved, the whole Congress was kidnapped and held hostage by one of the famous Sandinista commanders. All of the church properties, including the mission center—everything the Lord had given us the past ten years— were still in the name of Bob and Joan Tyson. After a short time in power, the Sandinistas began confiscating any properties belonging to a foreigner. Once again the people told us we would lose everything.

All of our property deeds had been left in a safety deposit box in the bank. We had the key, and we were the only ones who had the authority to open this box. There was no way we could get from Honduras to Nicaragua. Finally, we decided to send a key to Antonio Inestroza (he was the fourteen-year-old who was saved in our first meeting in Palacagüina). We wrote a letter of authorization to the bank and asked them to allow Antonio to open our box.

When Antonio arrived at the bank, he was informed that all of the safety boxes had been dynamited during one of the battles. When he showed them our letter, he was told that someone in the bank who knew us, had crawled on hands and knees through the rubble and had gathered up all the deeds (twenty-four in all), put a rubber band around them and was holding these in a safe place for us. He said if these deeds had fallen into the wrong hands, the Sandinistas would have known that all of these properties were owned by foreigners, and the properties would have been immediately confiscated.

We were told that one day a communist soldier stopped in front of the mission center and asked, "Who is the owner of this place?" A young girl, who was sweeping on the porch, in a very frightened tone replied, "I don't know. I think it is God." To this, the burly soldier gave her a dirty look, stomped his foot and got back in his jeep.

Bob had taught our national preachers not to get involved in politics: "God has called you to preach His Word." All knew that the Good Samaritan pastors were different. While other missions and churches were having all kinds of problems, even splitting among themselves, our pastors were preaching the Word and seeing many souls saved. While bombs were falling on one village, the Christians would flee to another village. But everywhere they went they were witnesses for Christ. The work flourished.

May 23, 1979, just two months before the Sandinistas won the war, forty-one people, including all of our pastors and their families, came across the border to visit us in Honduras. Missionaries Richard and Patty Comer and Darrel and Shirley Dean came for this reunion. The people began arriving early in the morning and kept coming until the middle of the day. Many were thinner than when we had last seen them. We listened as they told of the narrow escapes from death, of living under their beds as the bombs fell. Many tears of rejoicing were shed.

Have you ever enjoyed watching people eat? I fried chicken in our small camper for all of these people, and what a blessing to sit back and watch them eat, especially the little ones! Mrs. Petrona, the one who heard her friends and neighbors slaughtered, was still in a state of shock. She just sat staring into space as tears rolled down her face, but she didn't make a sound.

On May 25, all of the workers returned to Nicaragua, some to stay, others to arrange papers to go to other countries to preach. Antonio returned to bring back the mission truck and as much equipment as he could get out of Nicaragua. The next news we received was that the truck had broken down and the highways were destroyed. The next few weeks we spent in fervent prayer, begging God to have mercy on our national preachers and our multitude of friends who were trapped in this war-torn country.

29. Run Out Of Honduras

Thousands of refugees were pouring into Honduras every day to escape the war and the human slaughter going on in Nicaragua. We were able to rent the last available house in the city of Choluteca, and within days, some fifty-two people were living in this three-room house! Even though our family was sleeping in the camper, our days were spent either with the refugees or in trips to the border, waiting in vain to hear something from our pastors in the war-torn country of Nicaragua.

One day we were stopped at two roadblocks. At one we were given forty-eight hours to leave the country of Honduras; at the other, twenty-four hours. Because of the "tinted" windows in our van, our van was a threat, they said. We had not had any problems with this before, and many others had tinted windows.

Some people said we should stay and fight this, but if the authorities were telling us to get out, we felt we had better obey them. Already there had been two small battles near Choluteca, the town we were in, where rebels hideouts were found.

At the time we did not know the whereabouts of many of our people in Nicaragua, especially Antonio and his wife. As we drove up the road toward the United States, we felt as if we were forsaking them. The next day Antonio and Aminta came to Honduras by foot, leaving all of their material possessions behind.

Three days after we left Honduras, a house directly across the street from where we were renting was raided. Thirty Sandinista rebels were arrested, and large trucks of arms were carried out of the house. Once again God had gone before us, getting us out of harm's way. The Honduran government wanted nothing bad to happen to the North Americans; so we were safely on our way to the United States when this raid took place, still wondering why they were so upset with our tinted windows.

While in Honduras we were so burdened over the thousands of Nicaraguans sleeping on the streets or anywhere they could find. We knew people who had beautiful homes there; now they had nothing but the clothes on their backs. We looked for a place to rent in San Marcos de Colón, the border town. Finally we found a large, run-down old building that the government was renting as a technical school. They were teaching carpentry. Sawdust was ankle-deep. Three or four sewing machines were in one room where women were learning to sew. There was an outdoor toilet in the courtyard. The building was in bad shape, but it was big. We could clean it out and have room for many people to sleep. The owner, fearing the war was going to spread into Honduras, was selling this large building for only six thousand dollars. The only problem was, the government needed to use it because they said they had nowhere else to move.

When we arrived in the States after being told we had to get out of Honduras, a message was waiting for us from the owner of this building. The government had moved out, and the building was available. Bob immediately flew back to Honduras and purchased this building, which would house many refugees.

This building was purchased on July 14, 1979. The war ended a week later, and the refugees we had hoped to help returned home. Now we were left with an old run-down (empty) building in the town of San Marcos de Colón, Honduras. "Did we make a mistake, Lord? Did we spend Your money in vain?" we asked. If God had pulled back the curtain of time and given us just a glimpse of "things to come," perhaps we could not have stood it. Instead, He led us **step by step**, one day at a time, while we were seeking His will and trusting Him. God had His plans for that old run-down building, but it would be a long time before He showed them to us.

30. Work Begins In Honduras

Uncertainty prevailed as the new government was set up in Nicaragua. The unrest at the border between Honduras and Nicaragua was spreading throughout El Salvador and Guatemala.

Our pastors met us at the border and informed us that it was still unsafe for North American missionaries in northern Nicaragua. The Sandinistas put out information that North American missionaries were CIA agents. Although some of our pastors had been arrested and interrogated (some even spent time in jail) and were even accused of being informants for the CIA, these men stood firm on their profession of Jesus Christ as Lord and Saviour. Their "revolution" was actually the transformation of men's lives by the power of the Gospel.

Those who had been arrested were freed when no one could find that they were enemies to the new government.

We realized that the work would only operate by being one hundred percent national, led by Nicaraguans. Thank God for these faithful men who had been taught the Word of God and had been preaching for years.

On September 29, 1979, the troops moved out of the Good Samaritan Mission Center and turned this property back over to the Christians. A permit, signed by the new government, was given to the Good Samaritan Baptist Missions giving our nationals liberty to preach the Word of God in Nicaragua. A victory service was held in the streets of Condega, and a Bible march was held, with all the churches of the mission in attendance.

Their liberty to preach was never taken away. The churches were reporting record attendances, with people saved and baptized weekly. New churches were raised up. The church in Wiwili reported three hundred on International Bible Day, with a parade in the streets. One pastor reported forty-three baptized; another pastor reported twenty; another pastor reported five—all this under a communist government that had not yet openly declared that it was communist!

Brother Jorge Rizo, one of our national pastors from Nicaragua, felt led to stay in Honduras as a missionary, beginning services at the big building we had bought for refugees. He started with just his family, his Bible and his guitar. People passing by looked in the window, then walked on. One such young man was Julio Triminio. Julio didn't have any peace in his heart. Every time he passed that window and heard the singing, something would touch his heart, he said. Later, he went inside and listened. Then God began to deal with his heart. A few weeks later he was saved.

Julio has been a blessing down through the years. He not only is a preacher of the Gospel, but he has started mission churches. What a faithful servant for the Lord!

On a trip to the border to meet Antonio and Aminta and take an iron that they had left in San Marcos, Brother Jorge was arrested immediately for being a spy and was taken to the capital, where he was jailed for several days before anyone could find him. Meanwhile, both Antonio and Aminta were taken into custody when they rode up to the border on a motorcycle to pick up the iron. Antonio was taken into a small, air-conditioned room where his clothes were removed and where he was questioned for hours about working for the CIA. Unknown to him, in another room Aminta was being asked the same questions to see if there were any contradictions. Aminta knew what they were doing, and she prayed to God that she would say nothing that would cost Antonio his life. About dark, they were let go.

A few days later Jorge was found in a prison in the capital and was set free.

In October, Antonio wrote to us: "We were carried before an investigation committee to be investigated about our work. Everything went well, as Romans 8:28 tells us."

By the end of 1979, in the street meetings and in the new church started in San Marcos de Colón, Honduras, a total of ninety-five people had made professions of faith in Christ. We had bought airtime on a local radio station, and two messages were preached daily. **God was working in Honduras!**

31. Resident Missionaries In Honduras

Ever since the war in Nicaragua, we felt like we had lived in limbo. We visited churches in the United States, raising support for the national preachers who were going into other countries as national missionaries—Vidal Videa to Mexico, Favio and Paulino to Costa Rica, and many others. At every opportunity we made trips by land to visit Honduras, helping our two national missionaries there. Also, we would go almost daily to the border, hoping some of our Nicaraguan pastors would be there.

During this time, God had allowed us to spend six weeks in Puerto Rico, along with some of our national preachers, helping Missionary Charles Meek raise up a new work. Many young people were saved, and Maura Casco from Nicaragua stayed there to help Brother Meek and his wife in this new work.

Having seen on national television the multitude of "boat people" from Cuba—over a hundred thousand whom Castro had sent to the United States—Bob had a burden to preach the Gospel to these people. So we spent six weeks in Miami, Florida where the authorities gave us a gate at the Orange Bowl. There every night the Gospel was preached to those who had never heard. By this time, Maura had married a young Puerto Rican, and she and her husband worked with us in Miami, with Maura playing her accordion every night.

We had also helped Rich and Patty Comer in Mexico. Several of the national preachers from Nicaragua helped in these meetings. There were fifty-two professions of faith in Christ.

In all of these places, the Lord blessed, and we saw people saved. But our minds and hearts were never far from the place where God had called us to go.

In 1982, twenty-six national families were preaching in Nicaragua. New churches were continually being raised up, and souls were being saved and baptized weekly.

In Honduras, the work was now spreading out. Our national missionaries were doing the same thing that we had done in 1969 in Nicaragua––holding evangelistic campaigns, getting souls saved and baptized, and raising up churches. Needing a Bible school for preachers, they wanted Bob to come back and help them.

The end of December 1982 found us once again living in Honduras. We rented a house in Choluteca. It's difficult to describe how hot it gets in Choluteca, Honduras. A missionary came to see us. His wife asked, "What are you all doing living in the bat house?" We soon found out just what she meant. Every morning I woke up with bat droppings on my pillow. The attic was full of bats. Bob did everything he knew to get them out, but he never succeeded!

I would often hear something hit against my bedroom door. One afternoon when Stevie, about eight at the time, and I were trying to take a nap, we heard the noise. Looking toward the door, we saw a giant rat. It had finally succeeded in squeezing under the door and running toward the bathroom. It was probably trying to find water.

A neighbor told us that her little dog Nicky could kill rats, so we borrowed Nicky. We waited patiently for a visit from the rat the next day. Sure enough, it squeezed under the door. Nicky was on the bed with Stevie and me. Just as the rat made its way toward the bathroom, I put Nicky in its path. Nicky didn't want to tangle with that large rat, so she immediately jumped back on top of us. So much for Nicky and the rat!

In the midst of all the trials—bats, rats, intense heat, and rumors of another civil war all around us—once again God was working in our ministry just as He had done in the early days in Nicaragua.

32. The Man In The Cage

In 1981 a mission was opened up in the village of El Jicarito, Honduras, which at that time could only be reached by foot or horseback.

On August 3 we visited this area with some of our national preachers and a group of visitors from the United States. In a small community before reaching the mission, a vey old lady motioned to Bob from her doorway. He turned his horse in the direction of the door and approached her. With tears running down her cheeks, she asked very sincerely, "Isn't there anything you can do for my son?" She pointed across the small trail to a cage made of logs, and inside was a man they said was insane. He had been in this cage for almost eight years. Doubting that anything could be done for this wild, insane man, Bob told the mother that we were in a hurry to preach at a church service and he would talk to her later.

The Holy Spirit convicted Bob. This little mother was not a Christian, but she had heard that we were: "Surely these men of God could help my son." It bothered Bob, and all during the service he could hear her words, "Isn't there anything you can do for my son?"

On our way back, Bob and some of the national preachers stopped at the cage. Some of the Americans had picked up a "bug," and they were very sick with stomach cramps and nausea. I walked with them to the bus, which was parked at the main road, while Bob, and other national Christians stayed at the cage.

Bob believed this man in the cage was possessed with an evil spirit. He believed that if this man would call upon the name of Jesus as Saviour, the evil power would be broken.

So Bob and others prayed and begged him to plead the blood of Jesus Christ on his sins. At one point, it seemed that he would do so, but then some strange things happened. The man's face became grossly twisted; a mule tied close by, went into a pure panic, went up in the air and as he came back down, almost fell on Bob. The children ran and screamed, and vile talk began to flow from this man's mouth. He ran across the cage, sat down with his back to them and refused to look at or speak another word to them.

Finally Bob, and the others came to the bus feeling completely defeated but with a great burden for this man, bound and imprisoned by Satan.

We returned to the States with the group, but a few weeks later good news reached us by mail. One of our new preachers helping Brother José Santos wrote:

> Brother Bob, the Lord did something marvelous in the heart of the "crazy man" in the cage. I was on my way to have a service at the place where we rode horses when you were here. As I got off the bus at the main road, I became very sick. I was so hot I felt my clothes were sticking to me. I made it up to the cage and sat down to rest. I took out my Bible and began to read, and I prayed, asking God to help me,
>
> Suddenly, I felt a hand come out of the cage. In words that were easy to understand, the crazy man said, "Jesus is going to get me out of here." After I gave him the plan of salvation, he said, "I want to accept Christ as my Saviour." We both bowed our heads and prayed. He received the Lord as his Saviour.
>
> I called his mother and his brother, and both also accepted the Lord Jesus Christ as their Saviour. After this man had received Christ, he again said, "I have confidence that Christ is going to get me out of this place."

Praise God, it happened! He got out of the cage, and someone took him to the capital city of Tegucigalpa to be checked by the doctor.

Several months later in Honduras, Bob asked about the crazy man. "I heard he is out of the cage," Bob said, "but I want to see him."

"You'll see him tomorrow," replied José.

Sure enough, the next day Gilberto, the former crazy man, walked into our office in Honduras with a big smile on his face and gave a testimony of his salvation. Someone brought in an accordion, and he played for us.

For years the old empty cage stood as a testimony of God's power. We passed it many times as we made our way back to the church in El Jicarito. Now it's gone, but the memories going back to over 29 years ago are still fresh in our minds.

I asked one of our pastors the other day, if he knew whatever happened to Gilberto and he told me that he heard that he died in Tegucigalpa. He is in Heaven, but the memories of the wonderful work that God wrought in his life are still with us!

Joan Tyson

33. Another War In Nicaragua

March 14, 1983, we wrote:

> The eyes of the world are upon the situation between Honduras and Nicaragua these days. The anti-communists (Contras) are deep within Nicaragua, and according to the news here, they have taken over many towns. The newspapers report that there are 40,000 Nicaraguan people living in exile in Honduras. The anti-communist troops are made up of many ex-soldiers of the Somoza government and other Nicaraguans fighting to get their country back. The Sandinista government is accusing Honduras of helping these Contras.

Once again we found ourselves living in the midst of thousands of refugees. There was a shortage of food and water, and a drought besides.

It was not uncommon to see the roads filled with army tanks, trucks loaded with soldiers, Red Cross buses, etc. Roadblocks were set up everywhere. Almost daily we were stopped and searched. Coming from a service late one night, we were stopped in the middle of nowhere. Not a house was in sight. We were asked to get out of our car. If we had been sure these were real Honduran soldiers, we wouldn't have been so afraid, but many times these were Sandinistas who had infiltrated Honduras, using Honduran uniforms. I remember so vividly thinking that all of our family was going to be killed. Even Philip, who was about twelve years old and could speak the best Spanish in the family, began to tell the soldiers who we were and where we had been. They got in our car and searched everything, then said, "You can go."

There was a raging war on each side of Honduras— the Contras and Sandinistas in Nicaragua, and now the communists were trying to take over El Salvador. The only reason they had not succeeded in Honduras was the presence of the Contras and the strength of the Honduran government.

One Sunday morning we visited a new work that had been raised up in the town of Duyure. To our surprise, we found the pastor and a complete congregation from one of our churches in Nicaragua. They had fled over the mountain in Honduras. It was told that these Christians had given food to the Contras and, because of this, they had become enemies to the government. When the news reached them that the soldiers were coming to kill them, they all fled—all, that is, except the brother of the pastor, who told the rest to go on and he would be along shortly. He needed to check on his cattle. Weeks later, his bones were found— he had been tied to a chair, tortured and burned alive.

In spite of the threat of all-out war in Honduras, especially in the area in which we lived, God had not taken away our peace to work. He was blessing and opening up more and more villages for the Gospel to be preached. There were thirteen full-time students in the Bible school. Just about every day services were held in different sections of town: in the marketplace, on the streets, in the villages—anywhere there was an open door. We used the students in full-time service for the Lord. Just as Bob had done in Nicaragua, he taught and trained the Hondurans to carry the Gospel to their own people. The job was too great for one missionary.

34. Marriages In Honduras

In the early eighties, we learned that approximately eighty percent of all the adult population in southern Honduras were living together without marriage. Most of the men of the other twenty percent had other women besides their wives. The task before us was great.

Bob began to preach on fornication. The more he preached, the *sadder* the women got, and the *madder* the men got. This was messing up their playhouse! There was really no obligation on the man's part, and at any time he could move on down the road and "take up" with another woman. Even though I just knew one of these men would take revenge, Bob kept on preaching. The Holy Spirit began to work, and many of the men were saved. Even some who didn't get saved went before the judge and were married so their wives could be baptized and become members of the church.

In one church, the judge came and married ten couples. One couple among them was the parents of a pastor's wife. They had been living together for thirty years. That afternoon they were baptized in the river, and that night they said their vows in the church and dedicated their home to the Lord. What a sight as their children and grandchildren gathered around them! Remember too, all of these children were illegitimate in the sight of the law until their parents were legally married. They were then able to take their father's name. One of our pastors was able to change his name after his parents were married.

In one village, a young couple received Christ and went to the county seat to be married. To their surprise, the marriage book was clean—not even the judge was married. This young man was Ramon Aguirre, the first man to receive Christ in the village of El Naranjal. He has been a faithful servant of the Lord for many years.

I remember so well going with Bob to the town of Duyure, Honduras, many years ago. I wanted to start a ladies' circle in this new mission church. "We can't be officers, Sister Joan, because none of us are married. Will it be all right if we nominate our daughters?" And so they did!

Thank God for the power of the Gospel! Today this is one of the largest churches of Good Samaritan Baptist Missions in Honduras, with an average Sunday school attendance of over five hundred, including their missions!

The power of the Gospel was seen in the changed lives of the new believers. This has had a great impact in these towns and villages. The men and women who were married after living together for years set an example before their own children and neighbors of the change that the Gospel of Jesus Christ brings about when a person receives Christ as Saviour (II Cor. 5:17).

Years ago Bob was invited back into the mountains to marry a young couple that had received Christ in one of the mission churches. The journey by foot took all day. When they reached the little house where the wedding was to take place, Bob was surprised to find this young lady dressed in a white dress, along with her husband-to-be, and a multitude waiting for this very special event. As is the custom here, a regular church service was held first; then the marriage ceremony took place. Bob was most surprised when he was immediately surrounded by several men and women asking him to marry them also. "You don't understand," said Bob. "You have to have legal papers—a birth certificate and witnesses."

"We have all the papers," begged the people. "We've been saved, and now we want to get our lives in line so that we can be baptized." And so they were.

He married eight more couples in that humble little house way back in the mountains of Honduras. With their children gathered around—moms and dads, grandmas and grandpas promised the Lord to be faithful to one another until death.

I think the couple from our church in Los Mangos holds the record of being the oldest to get legally married. Brother Modesto was 88 years old and his "bride," Sister Petrona, was 76 when they were married by the judge and then a service was held in their home. They had been living together for 56 years. This brought out the entire village and people from other places. The little house would not accommodate the multitude of people who came to see this event. Later they were baptized, an outward showing of what had taken place already in their hearts. They are both still active in the church and Sister Petrona stays busy making jelly and gives a portion of what she makes to the church.

Several years ago, the judge from San Marcos de Colón came to the elderly center and married five elderly couples, who had been living together for many years outside of matrimony. I was careful to only invite the immediate families because I knew there would not be enough room at the elderly center for hundreds of people. I was surprised to see one of the announcers for Samaritan Radio along with his family, but more surprised when he told me that his grandparents were being married. Most of these precious old people are now in Heaven, but they, too, have left testimonies that will never be forgotten.

God gave us these very special experiences that we will never forget—seeing lives, homes and communities changed. And He is still changing lives. I was informed a few days ago that an elderly couple that eats every day in the "elderly kitchen" wants to get married. They both have received the Lord, and they want to be baptized—thirty-five years of living together, and now they're going to be married! All of this has come about by the power of the Gospel.

35. Feed The Hungry

Because of the civil wars in Nicaragua and El Salvador, more refugees were coming into Honduras every day, so the suffering increased. Hardly a day passed that there were not pleas for help from the poor and sick. Almost daily we witnessed processions walking behind little homemade wooden caskets on the way to the cemetery. Very early in the morning, mothers would bring their sick babies to our mission office. The majority of these were suffering from malnutrition and dysentery; some had polio and tuberculosis.

Bob was busy preaching and teaching daily in our Bible institute, so these people turned to me. Many of the women said they felt they could come to me for help because I too was a woman and a mother. A mother's heart for suffering children is something nothing can surpass. I could not take money designated to support our national preachers to help these people, but I never turned anyone away without trying to help. Somehow there was always a little money either to send them to a doctor or buy them medicine or food.

In Philip's schoolbook, I read one day about one of the great missionaries who had given all he had to help a poor, sick man. Later, he wondered what he would do for something to eat and why he had been so foolish to give away every cent he had. Then he came upon the words of our Lord in Proverbs 19:17: "He that hath pity upon the poor lendeth unto the Lord; and that which he hath given will he pay him again."

In November of 1983, God gave me an experience in the village of Azacualpa, Honduras, that changed my life. Bob had been invited to this village to preach on a Sunday morning. As always, I would teach the children. There must have been two hundred children under a large tree that morning. After the service, we were asked to stay and have another service in the afternoon, which Bob agreed to do. The pastor sent someone to buy us two hot Pepsi Colas (there was no electricity in the village), two cold tortillas and a can of sardines pickled in hot sauce. A little table and two little stools were put outside the hut where Bob had preached that morning, and this was where we were to have our Sunday meal.

As we sat there trying to figure out who would eat what—the sardines were so "hot," and we both suffered from colitis—my eyes were drawn to a little girl sitting just to the left of me under a large tree. She had taken a knife and was peeling a green grapefruit, but she never took her eyes off of me. I believe the Holy Spirit used that little girl that morning to speak to my heart and question: *Why does the missionary have a Pepsi, a tortilla and sardines, when I only have a green grapefruit? And why does the missionary have a pretty dress and shoes, and I only have underwear and am barefoot? Why does the missionary have a stool to sit on, and I only have the ground? Does Jesus love the missionary more than me?*

Probably none of these things entered the mind of that little girl that morning, but I believe the Holy Spirit used her to bring a truth home to my heart. I had taught all of those children that morning—and she was probably in the midst—that Jesus loved them and that He died on the cross and was raised from the dead. I told them that He had gone back to Heaven and was building a "great big house" for them (they had no idea what a mansion was), and someday He was coming back and would take everyone to Heaven who had received Him as Saviour.

My thought continued as I watched the little girl with her green grapefruit: *But what about* now? *Doesn't Jesus love me* now? *Doesn't Jesus want me to have food* now?

After the service that afternoon, I would leave that village of Azacualpa and return to my house where there was food. I would prepare a meal for my husband and my two sons—but what about all those children in Azacualpa with bloated stomachs, hair falling out and—*hungry*? I could leave them until the next time when we returned. I could again tell them how much Jesus loved them.

My life changed that day. The Lord used a half-naked little girl, peeling a green grapefruit while I feasted on tortillas, sardines and a hot Pepsi, to speak so strongly to my heart that I couldn't forget it. I told Bob I couldn't just minister to starving children—I had to do something. "Do what you feel like God wants you to do," he said. But what could I do? A whole country! We couldn't feed a whole country! *You can start with one*, a voice inside me whispered.

I would go to bed at night with feeding hungry children on my mind. I would get up in the morning thinking only of that. One day I sat down at the typewriter and wrote a letter to all of our sponsors. I simply shared my burden to feed hungry children.

In January of 1984, we visited Wrenn Memorial Baptist Church in Greenville, South Carolina for their annual jubilee. We arrived late on a Friday night and were sitting in the back when Brother John Everhart, the pastor, made this statement: "We receive a lot of letters from missionaries, every one of them with needs. But a few days ago I received a letter from Sister Joan Tyson that touched my heart. She wants to feed the hungry children in Honduras and we want to help her. Tonight our jubilee offering is going to 'Feed the Hungry'."

I received a check that night for $1000. During the month of January, I received a total of $2323.38.

I immediately called Honduras and gave them instructions to begin the first kitchen, with our national pastors in charge of this program. This would be a local church ministry. The pastors would find the children in their areas who were hungry and then find ladies in the church who would volunteer to cook the food. In the beginning I told them. "It doesn't matter if we have plates or spoons. They can eat off banana leaves with their fingers. Just get the food to them! And let them know that *Jesus* is sending them food, that He loves them and doesn't want them to be hungry." And so, the "Feed the Hungry" program started.

How little did I know in 1984 what "Feed the Hungry" would be in the Year 2009! Trusting God, we opened lunchroom after lunchroom, showing unconditional love to little boys and girls. The only requirement: hunger. Our churches began to fill with parents coming to see what kind of people we were—and hundreds of them have received the Lord. A director was put in charge in each kitchen and taught the little children about Jesus. They learned Bible verses and how to sing. And Jesus gets all the honor and glory.

We now have pastors who were saved in a "Feed the Hungry" kitchen. One of these is Pastor Danilo Hernandez, who was saved in the kitchen at El Triunfo, Honduras, when he was a little boy. He is now pastoring a church **filled with children**, and he has a "Feed the Hungry" kitchen, where more than 100 children eat daily. I don't think I have ever met a pastor with more patience towards children than Danilo has. He and his young wife both work with the children and are so thankful for this program.

Pastor Denis Vallejo was saved in the "Feed the Hungry" kitchen in El Naranjal, Honduras, when he was just a lad. Denis also had a sponsor in the "Opportunity" program. His mom and dad received the Lord and his Dad later became a deacon in the church. I can remember Denis' sponsors coming to see him and buying the family a milk cow. Denis pastors the church in San Fransisco, Honduras, and is married to one of the girls from this same village, who was sponsored and graduated from our high school. They also have a kitchen for the children in their church.

I wrote the following in a newsletter on February 1, 1984:

> **My heart is touched when I think of children going hungry, but my heart is also touched by the elderly who have no way of making a living. I can remember in the early days in Nicaragua when almost daily some elderly person would knock at our door asking for food. I would always think,** *What if this were my mother or daddy?* **I thank the Lord for a government that takes care of the elderly. In Honduras and Nicaragua this is not the case. If the old people don't have children to take care of them, then they have no hope.**
>
> **I thank the Lord that our program will enable us to help them a little. And only God knows how great our "Feed**

> the Hungry" program will be. If He can trust us to handle the money in the right way, then there is no limit to what He can do through you and me.

Just as God had burdened my heart for the hungry children, He burdened my heart for the elderly. But I didn't know what to do. Then God began opening doors. First, our people sought out the hungry and suffering; then we rented a house, and every day we sent out a van to bring them for a good meal. Just as in the children's kitchens, a director read the Bible to them and taught them to sing choruses and memorize Bible verses.

Soon many who could walk didn't wait for the van but came on foot and waited outside. I thought, *What if we had a center where they could stay all day—a place with a large porch and rocking chairs where they could rock and fellowship. It would have a big room with tables and chairs where they could play checkers or watch Christian videos.*

"Delight thyself also in the Lord; and he shall give thee the desires of thine heart" (Ps. 37:4). In San Marcos de Colón, Honduras, there is now a beautiful elderly center where the elderly can come early and stay late. If they are sick, we see that they get medical care and a hot meal every day. And, yes, there is a big porch with rocking chairs and a big room with a TV and tables for checkers! But the most important part is that the love of Jesus fills this place. They are not cooped up all day in a dark, dirt-floored hut, sick and hungry and alone. Now they can spend their days in a place filled with light, physically and spiritually. Just like the children, they are taught the love of Jesus. Many are in their eighties and nineties but still have good minds. They named their center "The New Beginning" because it is where they found love. Many have received Jesus as their Saviour. One can't be among these precious old people without feeling the presence of the Holy Spirit.

Over three thousand children and elderly people are able to eat one good meal a day. For many, this meal is all they get. This program is funded entirely by faith: no money is promised, but God always provides. "If He can trust us to handle the money in the right way, then there is no limit to what God can do through us" was written in 1984 when we started with forty-five children; today we feed more than three thousand, and more can be fed as the Lord provides.

"He that hath pity upon the poor lendeth unto the Lord; and that which he hath given will he pay him again."—Prov, 19:17

36. God's Work Continues Under Communism

The eighties were years of sadness and frustrations but also times of many triumphs and blessings. There was a time when it was almost impossible for any of our national preachers to leave Nicaragua. But someone would meet them at the border and get their reports of the work of the Lord.

The First Baptist Church in Palacagüina reported six hundred in attendance for their sixteenth anniversary service. It had been sixteen years since our first church was established in Nicaragua, but the memories were as yesterday.

The Sandinistas took over the little church in Wiwili, Nicaragua (remember where we slept with the spiders?), to be used for their command post. Carmen Carcamo was the pastor at that time. Bob urged him to come to Honduras because we were afraid Carmen would be killed.

Here is Brother Carmen's report from Honduras in July 1986:

> We got out the old tent this month for a campaign in Choluteca. When we looked at the tent, we remembered Brother Bob Tyson in Nicaragua using it from village to village and the thousands of souls that were saved in those days. We prayed to God to let us use it in the same way in Honduras.

On Bible Day, some three thousand marched in the streets of La Trinidad, Nicaragua, carrying banners and signs to celebrate the 413th

anniversary of the translation of the Bible into Spanish. The celebration ended with a tent meeting. Seventy were saved.

The national director in Nicaragua reported another sixty-one saved in a new area and a new church raised up. New churches were established in the villages of El Naranjal, Yusguare, and Choluteca, Honduras.

Brother Favio Videa reported that the work in Costa Rica grew 123% in 1986. God was blessing and protecting all of the pastors as they continued to go 'everywhere preaching His Word' (Acts 8:4).

March 1987 Bob wrote:

> **Right now we see the opportunity to have hundreds of national missionaries going into all parts of Central America preaching the Gospel. We liken them to an army waiting to be equipped for battle. The communists are making their bid. All we have to do is watch the news to see this. But WE have an opportunity to get these gospel preachers into Central America before the communists reach the people.**

We thank God today for over two hundred national preachers who still have the evangelistic spirit to win souls and raise up new churches for the honor and glory of the Lord! Our minds take us back to the verse in II Timothy 2:2:

"And the things that thou hast heard of me among many witnesses, the same commit thou to faithful men, who shall be able to teach others also."

37. Opportunity Of A Lifetime

One day in August 1987, Bob and I were visiting the kitchens in Honduras. School was in session, but none of these children we saw around the huts were able to go to school. School means buying books, a school uniform, shoes, and sometimes bus fare, depending on where you live. We discussed this situation. "They will never have an opportunity. They will grow up just like their parents—illiterate and poor. Someday, if sickness doesn't cause their death, they'll have only a little hut just like their parents. Communists will make a bid for them because the communists use poverty to convert people to communism, promising them an easier and richer life."

That day "Opportunity of a Lifetime" was born in our hearts and minds. A few months later it became a reality. We wrote to our friends and supporters:

> Bob and I have been in the Lord's work for twenty-three years, including the three and one-half years we spent at Tennessee Temple University and working in the mountains of Sherwood, Tennessee and in the mission of Snuffyville. Everywhere we have worked, God has brought so many wonderful children into our lives. Some of our national missionaries, now serving in five different countries, were just children when we first met them. We brought many of them into our home in Nicaragua and gave them an opportunity of a lifetime.
>
> In 1984 He gave the opportunity to start feeding the hungry children in Honduras. Our lives are now spent trying to help national missionaries and raise money for "Feed the Hungry."

Now another door is being opened. Most people would say, "You're doing enough. It's time to slow down. You're not as young as you used to be." Certainly the last statement is true. Our bodies tell us this quite often. But is there a place to stop or slow down? The Bible tells us to redeem the time, and we want to take advantage of the time God is giving us, for we know not how much time we have left.

Have you ever thought that you could give another person the "Opportunity of a Lifetime"; that you could make a difference in a child's growing up healthy and being able to get a job and not having to suffer as his/her parents have suffered? For $1.00 a day, a child's life could be completely changed.

For thirty dollars a month, a child could eat in the lunchroom and receive everything he needed to get an education—a school uniform, shoes, socks, and all the school supplies needed.

Never in our wildest imagination would we have ever dreamed that God was going to do what He did and is continuing to do throughout Honduras and parts of Nicaragua in the children's programs. When we began "Feed the Hungry," we never dreamed that someday there would be an "Opportunity of a Lifetime." How could we have ever dreamed that out of "Opportunity of a Lifetime," there would be Christian schools with more than two thousand students, that out of Christian schools there would be a need for intern or boarding students! On and on I could go.

A book itself could be written on "Opportunity of a Lifetime" and the fruit that has come from this program. Children and young people, who would have never had an opportunity to get out of the villages and dire poverty they were in, are now professionals working all over Honduras, Nicaragua, and even other countries. I have received phone calls and emails from young people now living in the United States and Spain who are serving the Lord. Some are now doctors, nurses, lawyers, teachers, office workers, and many went on to the military academy and graduated as officers. Two young people are working in the Presidential offices in the capital. All of this has happened because there are people who were willing to give one dollar a day to give an opportunity to someone else.

We never knew or ever planned for all of it to happen. But God did. He had a plan and a purpose for our lives. We were the ones "most unlikely to succeed." But with God, there are no failures.

The great missionary Hudson Taylor once said, "God's work done in God's way will not lack God's supply."

38. Christian Grammar School

Because God touched so many hearts, enough children were sponsored in San Marcos de Colón to begin our own grammar school in February 1989. This was not in our plans; we thought we would be sending them to the little public schools in the villages. But God had different plans.

We have never been ones to spend months in planning. When we feel that God wants us to do something and we have peace about it, we begin to work.

So it was with the beginning of a grammar school. Bob got peace about starting one just three weeks before school was to start. This meant we had three weeks to organize a school that would meet government standards and requirements, find teachers and, hardest of all, find a building.

We were about ready to give up when we were told about a building just a short distance from where we lived. The government, which had been using one side of it, was moving out. The other side was a cantina, and these people had no intentions of leaving. There was not another building for rent in town, and this one was our only hope. We began to pray. By faith, we rented the building and began to clean up our side.

As we worked, God worked! Three days before school began, this cantina operation moved out, and God's work moved in!

We worked frantically all night long painting, cleaning and hauling off liquor bottles and beer cans, getting it ready for inspectors from the

Department of Education who were coming the next day. And we were getting it ready for 180 precious children not only to receive the best in primary education but also to have classes every day in Bible.

Many children who started with us in the old cantina have now finished their education and are working in many different places in Honduras. It brings to mind the words of a medical doctor in San Marcos de Colón years ago: "One day San Marcos will be a different town. One day there won't be little street urchins eating out of trash cans because of love being shown to them by these Christians."

This doctor never lived to see the great difference the love of Christians could make in his hometown. But just before his death, he received the Lord and gave our son a part of a high mountain on which to put our first radio tower.

There is a great difference in every town and village where the love of Jesus has been shown. The little children still live in mud huts on dirt floors, but they come out every morning dressed in their school uniforms, pretty shoes and socks, with backpacks on their backs filled with everything they need to go to school. And they feel good! First of all, they know that Jesus loves them; also, that they have others in the United States of America who love them and share with them a part of that with which Jesus has blessed them.

Before their new school building was built, all of them had to pass in front of our house on their way to school. I can still see those smiling faces. They had no idea they were poor. They were receiving love—the greatest asset a person can possess.

I thank God that in our latter years He has brought into our lives such an exciting work of seeing little lives being changed and the old living out their lives in peace and happiness.

Had God shown it all to us when we first started out or even when we began the "Feed the Hungry" program, our hearts could not have contained it all. But He has done steps of miracles—step by step.

39. Christian High School

When we began the "Opportunity of a Lifetime" program, we had no idea there were hardly any high schools in the villages of Honduras. This meant that if a poor child could make it even through sixth grade, his education would end there. His parents could not pay for his room and board in some other city so he could further his studies.

So in 1990, one year after our grammar school opened, we found it necessary to begin a high school and to board our "Opportunity" children.

We began with just the seventh grade. Many pages could be written on the attacks from Satan as we tried to get a permit to open our Christian high school. I'll skip the problems and battles we faced except to say that once again God fought the battles for us.

We were trying to get a permit for just seventh grade, but the Lord used an ex-president of Honduras, whom our son had met, to get a permit for the entire high school. However, since time was running out, we only had time to prepare for seventh grade. In three days, forty-eight young people had registered. Classes began at the old mission center that we had bought years ago for the refugees.

Since most of our young people were coming from the villages, this opened up a new ministry for us—that of boarding students. We would be responsible for these seventh graders twenty-four hours a day. What a change it was for them—indoor bathroom, running water, electricity.

Do you remember the village where the "Feed the Hungry" program was started? Young people from there proved to be our most intelligent students. Their minds had not been cluttered with television and the junk of this world, and they were anxious to learn. Later, when we began to receive students from all over Honduras, including sons and daughters of doctors, lawyers, and parents who had been able to give their children the best, guess who excelled in grades! **Our "Opportunity of a Lifetime" students!** It was not always true, for some were affected by a lack of food and sickness in their very young years, but the majority were quick learners.

I could write a book on our new family of teenagers, which was the beginning of a new generation the Lord was allowing us to see raised up in Honduras to be used for His honor and glory.

I used to ask myself, *Why are the enemies of the Gospel so against our having Christian schools?* We had no facilities—just a rented cantina building for the grammar school and an upstairs room in an old building for the high school. We became firm believers that Satan knows the future, since he worked in every way to stop these schools, knowing that thousands of young people would pass through Good Samaritan Schools and leave there with their lives changed forever.

Bob once compared our high school to a beautiful rose garden with the roses all in bloom just waiting to be picked. How we thank the Lord that He sent all these beautiful, young, tender "roses" our way to be taught the Word of God and let us see them transformed into shining lights for the Lord Jesus Christ.

In Honduras, the basic classes actually end with ninth grade, at which time the students choose their career, and the next two to four years are devoted to preparing for just that. The Department of Education gave us a permit to teach Bachelor in Computer (a three-year course), Bilingual Secretarial program (a four-year course), Bachelor in Science and Letters (a two year course), and Commercial (a three year course).

Our graduates have no problem getting jobs. Those poor children who once had no future are now working all over Honduras and Nicaragua.

Not only does "Opportunity of a Lifetime" give an opportunity to the children, but it also has given jobs to many people. For example, we gave work to the local women to make the hundreds of uniforms. And so, in the same building that was bought years ago for refugees, we opened up a sewing center where all the school uniforms are now made. We needed cooks, counselors, guards, maintenance men, and interns for the high school. This meant more jobs for the people.

God has truly taken the 'weak things to confound the mighty' (I Cor, 1:27). Remember the doctor who said that one day San Marcos de Colón would be a different place? It *is* different!

The high school is no longer in the old mission building but in a beautiful Spanish-type "fort" which has attracted hundreds. They come to see this beautiful architecture. Alongside the high school is a brand-new grammar school, which our children prayed into existence. We began each project with no money, and at the end of every week there was enough money to pay for that week. God provided, and when the construction projects were complete, not a cent was owed. That was a miracle, but our God is a God of miracles.

40. Growing For Jesus

The early 1990s were years of phenomenal growth in every area of the mission. God was continuing to call more and more young men into the ministry. In 1991 thirty-three students were enrolled in the Bible school in Honduras and twenty-seven in Nicaragua. New churches were being started all over Honduras and Nicaragua.

May 9, 1992, the Good Samaritan Baptist High School building was inaugurated. A burning desire in Bob's heart to build a "fortress" representing God's power to withstand and defeat the enemy, Satan, in the lives of Honduran young people had become a reality.

A small army of boarding students was now coming from all over Honduras and parts of Nicaragua. As the fame of Samaritan High School grew, more and more parents were sending their teenagers to us. "Where will we put all these young people?" we asked ourselves. We should have known better than to worry or fret when the work is of the Lord. The same God who entrusted these young lives into our care would supply all our needs according to His riches in glory.

God burdened the hearts of two very dear friends, Doyle and Margaret Gunter, to buy a farm for us only about two miles out of San Marcos. We remodeled the old house on this seven-acre farm. Here the young men would live, study and learn about growing their own food. God touched the heart of one of our young preachers, a Bible school graduate. He and his wife moved in with these young boys to be their dorm parents.

Our young girls continued to live at the mission center, but soon a decision had to be made—turn students away or build dormitories for them? How could we turn anyone away? You probably already know the answer.

Shortly after our high school was finished, and without any money, we started construction behind the high school. As in every construction project, we paid as we went. No money was promised by our supporters, but God always sent it in. Today there is a beautiful two-story building which houses up to two hundred girls downstairs and has classrooms, a sewing academy and rooms for guests upstairs. When this was finished, not one cent was owed. "How?" you ask. The only answer I can give is, "It's a miracle!"

In the early 1990's we were feeding two thousand a day in the "Feed the Hungry" kitchens. Every time we visited a home and saw children waiting for leftover food, we just added on more children to our kitchens.

Nothing can bring more joy and thrill to a Christian's heart than seeing God work. And how He did work in our lives! Whatever we needed for His work, He supplied—not all at one time but just when needed—and one step at a time.

41. Artesian Well

"They're cutting off our water." No sadder words were ever spoken, especially if you're housing one hundred boys who need water for survival!

The farm that God gave us was wonderful. The boys had plenty of room, and everyone was happy, but then came the news. We were using too much water, so the water was cut off.

Bob went to see the lady in charge in this small community. First of all, she didn't like "gospel believers"; second, "You're using too much water." The community water came from a tank on the side of the mountain. After trying to convince her that we had one hundred boys living there and we had to have water, she agreed to turn the water on for two hours a day. Well, two hours is better than nothing. We didn't know that the hours would be from 7:00 a.m. to 9:00 a.m. Our boys left for school at 6:45 a.m. That meant no water to bathe with and no rest rooms.

"Is this what You want, God? Is this Your will?" Bob fervently asked God.

"Drill a well," he seemed to hear a voice say. Drill a well? We didn't even know there were any well drillers in that part of the country.

We found a well driller; and after making the arrangements (checking prices, etc.), operations began. Remember, we never have any money to start anything, so this well was a new adventure and strictly by faith. But in a hundred or so feet we would have a well, and that would take care of the problem—we thought.

One hundred…200…300…365…and nothing! By this time we were already in debt (around seven thousand dollars), and no water. To make matters worse, the well driller said, "We are drilling in a red rock where there is hardly ever any water found." Then he asked, "What do you want me to do?"

"It's time to do some more praying," answered Bob. He stopped everything until the next day.

"We're in big trouble," Bob told me as he explained what was happening. Quickly I faxed a letter to our supporters asking them to pray, explaining how much in debt we were already and with almost no hope of finding water.

During the night, Bob awakened on three occasions after hearing something or someone speak to his spirit, saying, "Twenty feet more." (It does not have to be in an **audible** voice that God speaks to His children.)

The next morning he made his way back out to the site. The well driller was waiting. "Well, Preacher, what is your answer?"

"We're going down twenty feet more," Bob said.

"Did you say twenty feet more?" the well driller asked. "Why just twenty feet? Where did you come up with that amount?"

Bob answered without hesitancy, "Because God told me."

The well driller didn't know what to do with that, so he simply stated, "It's your well—it's your money. I'll go down twenty feet; then I'll stop." And so he did.

"You still have no water, Preacher," he announced, "but I'll finish my end of the bargain. I'll put the pipe in and fix it just like you have a real well of water, but you have no water."

"I'll have it if God wants me to have it," Bob answered.

The next morning Bob and I went out to see if the well driller had finished. As we neared the property, the first thing I saw was water running down the Pan American Highway in front of the boys' dorm! It had covered the ditches and the yard of the house. We got out of the car in amazement!

"What in the world is going on?" Bob turned to the mountain where the community water tank stood and remarked, "You turned our water off; now God has busted your tank!" We really thought their tank had burst and spilled the water down the mountainside.

No, God didn't burst their tank; He gave us an artesian well! During the night, the water had begun to rise almost three thousand feet up in the mountains—almost unheard of—and it began to pour out the top of our 385-foot well! Without a pump, it produced 14,400 gallons in twenty-four hours! And it came out lukewarm. Now the boys wouldn't have to bathe in ice-cold water!

What about the cost? Once our letter reached the United States, God's people not only sent enough to cover the expense of the well, but enough was left over to finish the upstairs construction on the boys' dorm!

"We have a well of living water," we wrote our sponsors on February 21, 1994. Almost sixteen years later, this well is still running over! People have come from all over southern Honduras to see the first artesian well in southern Honduras.

And the lady in charge of the water system—well, she sent engineers to see exactly how all of this came into being. When they asked Bob how he knew just where to drill the well, they left even more confused when he answered, "God showed me were to put it."

This well today furnishes water not only for the boys' dormitory, but for our home and the home of Pastor Mario Sanchez and his family, who live on the property; also for a ten-room, motel-style building for visitors; for the tabernacle and Bible institute across the highway, and when no one is using water, it drains into a pond behind the boys' dorm that Bob had dug to take care of the excess water. **To God be the glory!**

42. Radio Ministry

"Dad, I want to build a radio station." At first we thought Philip, then age twenty-one, was kidding. We were sitting on our back porch in our rocking chairs when he approached us. One look told us he was not kidding.

"Son, do you realize what kind of money you are talking about?" Bob finally asked. "You're talking about thousands and thousand of dollars." We had no response to Philip's next words, "But, Dad, you have always lived and done everything by faith." What could Bob say to that? His son had seen that in his dad's life; now he was convinced that the Lord wanted him to build a radio station.

We had always believed in the power of radio. One of our first ministries in Nicaragua was a daily thirty-minute program on a secular station. That's how the man in Light of the Jungle church heard the Gospel and was saved, which had convinced us even more that the Gospel could reach areas that the missionary would never be able to reach. In Honduras, we had two thirty-minute programs on a secular station, but now our son was talking about the mission having its own radio station. *Impossible*, we thought.

A few months later, sitting on the same back porch, we watched as donkeys carried equipment for the tower up the trail to the top of the mountain! I think a book could be written just about the radio ministry; how God touched a colonel's heart at the last hour to sign a permit for a frequency; how God touched the heart of a doctor, who wasn't even saved at the time, to give Philip the top of his mountain on which to put the first tower; and how Philip was able to raise the money for the first FM station in the town of San Marcos de Colón.

Imagine how we felt at 6:00 a.m., September 28, 1991 upon hearing Philip's voice as he read God's Word on the Good Samaritan radio station!

As soon as this station was completed, work began on an FM repeater tower, this time on one of the highest mountains in Southern Honduras, called Bañaderos, near the town of Pespire. With this 240-foot tower, the Gospel could be heard not only in Honduras but also in neighboring El Salvador—91.9 FM.

Realizing that many of the country people did not have FM radios, the third repeater tower, 1230 AM, was put up in the Choluteca Valley area. It was while this tower was being built that Philip began to have headaches so severe that sometimes he passed out from the pain.

1995: Philip had been given an FM frequency in the state of El Paraiso, which has a population of 800,000. The tower was being put up in the city of Danlí, the capital of El Paraiso. After issuing the permit, the government had given 120 days to start construction: if not started, the frequency would be lost. Philip had waited on this permit for fifteen months.

In the middle of the construction, March 1, 1995, Philip suffered the first series of mini-strokes. He was hospitalized in the capital city where tests showed that he had had a total of five strokes in his brain. Three were very small transient strokes, but two, a little bigger, had temporarily paralyzed the left side of his body. He was sent from Honduras to Emory Hospital in Atlanta, Georgia. For six days some of the best doctors in the world studied and treated him. All were fascinated when they heard of his missionary work and how, at the age of twenty-five, he was building his fourth radio station.

The doctors at Emory confirmed what the doctor in Honduras had told us—this was a very rare type of migraine, and the excruciating pain was causing the strokes. Philip was told that it was very dangerous for him to be under stress, but from the hospital bed he planned to build more stations.

November 1995: The Danlí station was now on the air.

A donation was received to build a radio station in Nicaragua. Land had to be bought for the tower, but the studios were housed in the same old building where Philip and Stevie grew up—our mission center that years before had been taken over by the communists.

The devil waged an all-out attack against the building of this station. All types of vandalism occurred, threats were made to burn down the studio, and on and on. On the night before the day the inspectors were to come, the electrical poles near the tower were sawed in two. Philip, the engineer and the faithful preachers in Nicaragua worked all night. At dawn the mayor loaned them a truck to go to the capital to buy more poles. A few months later, the battle was won, and the fifth radio station of Good Samaritan Baptist Missions was on the air— 1350 AM.

Five years—five powerful stations beaming out the Gospel eighteen hours a day, seven days a week. It sounds like it was easy, just one station after another—no problem. Oh, yes, there were many problems, and I suffered every time my son suffered. But his faith and determination throughout this time were such an inspiration to me.

The headaches really never left him; so on Wednesday, December 3, 1997, Philip walked into our house and said, "Dad, I can't go any further. My head feels like ten pounds are sitting on every strand of hair. I want you to keep the radio stations going for the Lord.

Philip's ministry in the radio ended, but his fruit remains. All one has to do is drive throughout Honduras and northern Nicaragua and see all the towers standing tall and beaming out the Gospel of our Lord Jesus Christ.

From the beginning we knew that if these radio stations were to continue, it would be a miracle. We had no experience running radio stations; but come to think of it, we never had experience in any of the areas God put us in! We just offered ourselves to Him, and he did the rest.

God burdened the heart of our youngest son, Steve, to head up Samaritan Radio.

A permit for a station, 1090 AM, in Tegucigalpa had been purchased by Philip in 1999. He only had a small transmitter and was operating this from his home. When Stevie took over the management of Samaritan Radio, his desire was to move the studios to the capital city of Tegucigalpa. I doubted this would ever be done because of the great expense in moving this station. I thank the Lord for the faith of my sons, which they had always seen in their dad. It took one year for this to be completed, and in 1991 Samaritan Radio went on the air with a 10,000-watt station broadcasting from the capital city. Four acres of land had been bought on a mountain called Canto Gallo with two antennas installed—a 220 ft. and 120 ft., enabling over two million people in the central parts of Honduras and Costa Rica to hear the Gospel.

In 2003, after renting for one year, the Lord allowed the mission to buy a house in Tegucigalpa and completely remodel it to house the main operations of Samaritan Radio, including recording and production studios.

In 2004, the seventh station, 1340 AM, was built in the city of Comayagua, which was the first capital of Honduras. A 200 ft. tower gives this station a potential listening audience of approximately one half million people.

In 2005 an eighth station was built on the northern coast of Honduras in the city of La Ceiba, a population of approximately one half million enabling this station to reach the country of Belize.

On August 10, 2006, a 103.5 FM station went on the air in Tela, Honduras. This covers an area of about 300,000 people and completes all of the basic territory of the northern coast of Honduras and different parts of Belize.

Under Stevie´s direction, not only have new stations been built, but in every station the transmitter power has been raised and more powerful solid state transmitters bought. At the present time, a 12,000 watt Nautel solid state transmitter is being installed in the capital city.

Over the years, a harvest of souls have been reaped through the Samaritan Radio Network. It is amazing the number of telephone calls received daily, in addition to letters. Souls have been saved in the U.S. and others countries through internet. Just in the last three years, over 25,000 have called or written that they have received the Lord.

Samaritan Radio Network has come a long way since the day Bob and I watched the little donkeys taking the equipment up the mountain in San Marcos de Colon, Honduras. But this shows what our God can do. **There is nothing impossible for Him.**

43. Water In Marcovia, Honduras

In the nineties our national pastors continued preaching the Word everywhere the doors were opened. The radio stations were bringing in hundreds of letters and calls from towns and villages all over Nicaragua, Honduras, and El Salvador. In the large city of Danlí, Honduras, it was said that everyone listened to Samaritan radio. A national preacher was sent to Danlí, and a church was started. Appeals for a preacher to come and preach were coming from many places, and they "went everywhere preaching the Word." From the humble beginning when Bob taught one seventeen-year-old boy on our front porch every morning in 1969, God had raised up an army of preachers who were willing to go anywhere at any time to preach the Word of God.

In almost every place, the services began in a new believer's home, but in just a few weeks, there would be no more room. And places large enough to accommodate the people were too expensive to rent. Since we had no mission representatives in the United States, the responsibility was on Bob's shoulders to raise the money, to build church buildings and help the national preachers go as missionaries.

One such place was Marcovia, Honduras. We compared Marcovia to the man fallen by the way. The priest and Levite passed him by, but the Samaritan showed compassion, giving all he had to help the stranger.

On our first trip to Marcovia, we saw nothing but a desert place filled with suffering people. We asked ourselves, *How do these people survive?* One of our national preachers who had moved there with his wife had put up a little two-room mud hut and was holding services in his house. There were no pews, not even a pulpit, but we found many dear people there who came out to hear God's Word. Later on, when the church in Azacualpa was blessed to have a new building, they donated their old lumber to Marcovia. Now the people had a stick-and-plank church with open sides, a few handmade benches and a roof to protect them from the sun and rain.

Several months later when a church group visited us, God burdened their hearts to build a church for these people. However, before construction started, God burdened Bob's heart about an even greater need—water. There was no water: the people were living in a desert and starving to death. On a Sunday morning, we met with the people and let them decide. "Do you want a church building, or do you want water?" Bob asked. One by one they stood and said, "Brother Bob, we will die without water. We can use this building to worship the Lord."

We contacted Pastor Quinn Evans and the Pleasant Grove Baptist Church in Hiram, Georgia, who had donated the money for the new church building, explaining the situation. We asked if we could use the money to drill a well for these people. Brother Quinn assured us it was all right. So a well driller came in, and God blessed with an abundance of water. The cost was five thousand dollars. We sent Stevie with a check to pay the bill and he could not believe what he heard, "No charge." God had already prepared the heart of the well driller. He had seen God give us an artesian well (he was the same driller), and he wanted to get in on God's blessings. All he would say was, "I made a promise to God…"

A transformer and electrical wires were bought to run electricity to the church, a pump and pipes were bought for the well, and still there was enough money left over to build the church.

For years this well of water that God provided has served the whole community.

A few weeks after everything was finished, we drove down the dusty road to Marcovia. Suddenly there appeared this pretty white church, and behind it were little houses made of sticks, mud, paper, or whatever the people could get. The tears began to flow as we saw this as a picture of our dear Lord standing in front to protect and provide, just as a mother hen does for her chicks. Out to the side, a well was there to satisfy the physical thirst. But the greatest of all was the water of life, which He had already so freely given so all would never thirst again.

44. Hurricane Mitch

October 1998: Honduras and Nicaragua were hit by a hurricane that almost destroyed both countries. It was reported that every major bridge was heavily damaged or destroyed. Many towns and villages were completely cut off from the world, including San Marcos de Colón, home of our mission center in Honduras.

At the time the hurricane hit, Bob and I, along with a group of pastors and young people form Honduras, were visiting churches in the United States. For several days we were unable to contact anyone, including our own sons who were in the capital city, the place where most of the people lost their lives.

As soon as possible, we returned to Honduras. We couldn't believe what our eyes were seeing. In one section of the city of Choluteca, the tractors were at work trying to remove tons of dirt higher than the houses. We had to keep our windows closed because of the horrible smell. Hundreds died in this one area. No one thought the hurricane would reach this far, so no one was prepared. Entire families were buried under large mounds of dirt.

"The rich and poor cried together." We heard this over and over from our national preachers who worked with the people— praying with them, consoling them and trying to give comfort from God's Word. Natural disasters show no respect for people. Everyone is affected—the poor and rich alike!

On a Sunday afternoon we drove as far as we could in our jeep, then walked for two hours up a mountain, crossing foot logs and rivers that once were small branches, to reach a public schoolhouse which was the only building standing. This was being used to house all the refugees. Already two big pots of beans and rice were cooking over an open fire. The beans and rice had been taken in by our national preacher. We talked to the refugees about Jesus, assuring them that He loved them and would provide for them. And He did.

Some 150 of our high school students who lived at the school were trapped there during the hurricane. Until the roads were opened, the only food they had was corn that Bob had planted on the mission farm, which now lay beaten in the mud. What could be saved was picked from the ground and brought to the high school where the students shelled the corn for tortillas.

The hardest damage to our mission property was in Nicaragua, where several church buildings, pastoriums, and many houses of the believers were completely washed away. God, through His people, helped us to build eighty-four little houses and provide for months for His people in Nicaragua and Honduras. Several new "Feed the Hungry" kitchens were opened. It was amazing to see God touching the hearts of unknown people to send offerings so we could help these in distress.

'Who can separate us from the love of God?' During our years as missionaries here in Central America, we have seen droughts, famines, floods, earthquakes, and hurricanes, but nothing has separated us from God's great love. **'He is God, and beside Him, there is no other.'** What good could have come out of a hurricane that almost destroyed two countries? If nothing else, it showed people here, especially Christians, His great love for them as manifested through Christians from all over the world who provided for them during this terrible time. Whatever God chooses to do to us, through us or for us, we can still say, **"To God be the Glory!"**

45. Another Miracle Of God

Looking down at Bob on a hospital bed in Tegucigalpa, Honduras, a doctor made this statement: **"I am looking at a miracle of God."**

On August 4, 1999, at 11:00 a.m., Bob suffered a massive stomach hemorrhage. He had visited my English class at the high school; as we were leaving the classroom, he began to feel dizzy. We sat down to see if it would pass, but then he had difficulty breathing. He began to have pain in his chest, and he was going in and out of consciousness. I though he was having a heart attack. Luz, our housekeeper, and two more ladies were just a couple of rooms away preparing some of the girls' dormitory rooms for visitors coming the next day. The four of us were able to get Bob to one of the beds. Then came nausea, then dysentery, and then blood. But oh, how good and merciful God is!

We live in a small town, three and a half hours from a good hospital. What went on at the Good Samaritan high school for the next three hours is indeed a miracle from God! When the doctor arrived, the first thing he did was to give Bob a shot in the vein, which he said would send oxygen to the brain.

I didn't even know such a shot existed. While teachers led hundreds of students in prayer, everyone was working frantically to keep Bob alive. I will never forget the love and care shown by so many people, especially the young doctor in this town who had so little with which to work.

Three hours later, at 2:00 p.m., Bob was laid on a mattress in the back of our van for the three-and-a-half-hour trip to the hospital in Tegucigalpa. With Antonio beside him and Stevie driving, he continued to vomit blood during the long trip. At around 6:00 p.m., they arrived at the Viera Hospital where two specialists were waiting in the emergency room. Five days later, one of the specialists made the statement, which I quoted before: "I am looking at a miracle of God." He went on to say that if a young man living close to the hospital had suffered the same thing, it would still have been a critical situation. But for a sixty-five-year-old man living in a faraway village to suffer a massive hemorrhage and make it to the hospital over six hours later, especially over the roads we had to travel, was a miracle of God!

Never have we seen such an outpouring of love and concern. The news of Bob's illness reached into Nicaragua and even Panama, and men whom Bob trained thirty years before came all the way to Honduras to see him and tell him how much they appreciated all he did for them in the early years of our ministry. Miguel Rivera from Managua, Nicaragua, the same seventeen-year-old boy whom Bob taught on our front porch over thirty years before, made this statement: "Brother Bob has worn his body out in the work of the Lord."

Our national pastors here in Honduras were equally concerned. "You don't have to preach or do any other work. We'll do all the preaching. We just need your presence, your counsel, your encouragement," they said. So many of these men of God had been with us since they were very young. They lived in our home for years in Nicaragua where Bob taught them every day. They had been faithful throughout the years. Now they were begging God to let Bob stay longer with them.

46. A Year of Growth and Change

The pastors prayed that God would let Bob stay longer with them—and the Lord let Bob live for eight more precious years and the pastors worked and preached with more fervor and zeal than ever. We know they were doing it for the Lord but at the same time they were showing Brother Bob that his labor bestowed upon them had not been in vain.

For the next few years, we witnessed a growth in all of the work that we never dreamed possible. God blessed every ministry of Good Samaritan Baptist Missions. Many new Feed the Hungry kitchens were opened in needy areas all over Honduras. New churches were established, too many to name, constructions of new church buildings, kitchens, and pastoriums could be seen all over Honduras and Nicaragua. Our schools had record attendances. A new kindergarten and grammar school was opened in San Luis, Santa Barbara, Honduras.

In the years 2004, 2005 and 2006, more than 9,000 souls professed Christ as Saviour just in the churches. Thousands called in to be saved or wrote that they had received Christ through Samaritan Radio.

One of our pastors was invited by a Colonel to preach at the large army base in Choluteca, Honduras, which eventually led to weekly services; then a church was built directly in front of the base. Hundreds of soldiers have been saved and left this base for different areas of Honduras.

God allowed us to build a beautiful tabernacle in Comali, Honduras which would seat some 1500 people, a building that has attracted people all over Central America. The grammar school in San Marcos de Colon was built during this time and, as always, the Lord provided every cent. The old mission center was rebuilt in Condega, Nicaragua which now houses our offices, a large auditorium for special meetings, and the Good Samaritan Christian schools. Vidal Videa's ministry in Mexico grew to several churches with local pastors pastoring these churches. There were five churches in Costa Rica under the leadership and ministry of Paulino Benavides.

Writing this chapter has brought back memories that have touched me emotionally more than any other chapter. As I remember all of these marvelous works that the Lord did during this time, it almost seems like a dream. Many thought that when Bob got sick and could not travel nor visit churches in the United States to raise money, that this Mission would fall. But we were all taught a very special lesson. God´s work does not depend on one man or one woman. God provided and touched hearts to help us in ways that can only be described as MIRACLES.

Not only were there constructions going on everywhere but also five more radio stations were built and more powerful transmitters bought for the older stations. Thousands of souls were saved through the preaching going out on Samaritan Radio, which was now reaching into five countries and, also by Internet. Twelve new telephone lines were installed to take care of the vast number of people calling in from everywhere to receive Christ. Calls came in from the United States, Spain, Mexico, and other countries saying they were saved listening by Internet. We only know about the thousands of phone calls received but what about the majority of people who do not have telephones. Only in heaven will we know....

This was also a period of change. As servants of the Lord, we never know what He has in store for our lives. After 32 years of serving the Lord with the Good Samaritan Baptist Missions, Antonio Inestroza, felt led to move to the United States to begin a ministry with the Spanish speaking people. He began working with the Victory Baptist Church in Thorsby, Alabama. Antonio had been with us since he was 15 years old. We saw him grow up, marry Aminta, who was saved in our second tent meeting in Nicaragua in 1970, have five beautiful children, one of whom is married to the son of Pastor Donald Jones, pastor of Victory Baptist.

In the years 2004 and later, we had mountains to climb and valleys to cross but the Lord never left us. During the hard times, that is when we felt His presence the most. Things happen in our lives that we don´t understand, but we find that we have the greatest peace when we don´t try and understand—but just accept and remember that we belong to the Lord. He saved us many, many years ago and later called us to be missionaries. We don´t try and understand why Bob Tyson, who, as one doctor said, has worn his body out for the Lord, is now losing his memory and soon won´t even be able to remember his walk with God during all these years in Central America. We just try and accept it and remember that Brother Bob belongs to the Lord.

When groups come and see all the beautiful buildings, the churches, the feeding centers, the schools, and all the MARVELOUS WORKS the Lord has done, they know that they are witnessing Miracles from God. This has always been our desire. We want the Lord to be Exalted and Lifted Up. We want people to see what He can do if only we will give our ALL to Him.

Most of all, whatever we do, we want it to be done for the Honor and Glory of the Lord.

47. "Via De Victoria" Tabernacle Dedication

"And the Lord said unto David my father, Whereas it was in thine heart to build an house unto my name, thou didst well that it was in thine heart." I Kings 8:18

Thursday, April 17, 2003, was one of the greatest highlights in the ministry of Good Samaritan Baptist Missions---the dedication of the new tabernacle in Comali, Honduras.

It took three years to build and at the end of every week, the Lord had the money for us to pay all the bills for that week. When the tabernacle was finished, it was paid for. TO GOD BE THE GLORY, GREAT THINGS HATH HE DONE!

Everything went far beyond any expectations we might have had, including the multitude of people who came for the dedication. Seventeen buses, 9 large trucks, vans, small trucks, cars and people walking, brought an estimated 3000 people to this very special service. The building quickly filled, the balcony and even the steps leading to the balcony were filled with people. Every door was filled with people who couldn't get in—they were looking in every window. Outside there were hundreds who could only hear. Never in our wildest imaginations did we think there would be this many people. It took everyone by surprise, even our pastors. Probably the ones most surprised were the cooks who had cooked half the night, preparing large vats of chicken and rice for **1500 people.**

As I walked around the building seeing all these people who couldn't even get in, I thought of the beginning of our ministry in the early 1970's when most Evangelical churches were just little mud huts somewhere on the back streets. People were taught back then by the religious leaders that we were "chanchos" (hogs in English) and that Gospel believers were ignorant and could only work with the ignorant and poor people. I remember Bob saying in those days that he wanted to build beautiful buildings for the Lord **and on the front streets!** God has honored his desire to do this because over the years beautiful buildings have been built, but nothing like this tabernacle on the Pan American highway. Our grandson, Philip, Jr., made a beautiful statement, "Grandma," he said. "This looks like Jesus' house because everything is so white". We want the world to know this is "Jesus' House" here on the Pan American highway bordering Nicaragua.

Stevie and Bob cut the ribbon, and with Stevie holding his dad's hand, they marched in together. Later Stevie spoke and then dedicated a song to his dad, **"THE ANCHOR HOLDS,"** while both sat and cried. It was a very touching moment. Bob was unable to say anything during the service but the expression on his face showed that he was deeply touched.

His prayer had been that God would let him live to see this tabernacle dedicated and God was allowing it. This was his last project. Even though his health was failing, still he would make his way to the tabernacle and if there was something he didn't like, he would make them tear it down and do it like he wanted it. In the beginning, the walls had to be torn down. I can remember on more than one occasion, he would shake the staircases and just shake his head. Finally, he couldn't stand it anymore and he said, "Tear them down!" And they did! Both staircases were torn down and rebuilt. It was like God was giving the orders and Bob was carrying them out. Everything had to be perfect.

We never spent a cent on an architect drawing up plans. Bob had it all stored in his mind and God had sent us a construction man, about 5 feet tall, who seemingly could take this out of Bob's mind. I have seen Bob drawing in the dirt and Don Manuelito could take his drawings out of the dirt and build beautiful and unique buildings. This is what happened with the tabernacle.

One of our guest speakers for the dedication was Pastor Neil Eidson from the Victory Way Baptist Church in Hillsville, Virginia. It was Victory Way that began this great project with the first donation, and for this reason it was named **"VIA DE VICTORIA,"** Victory Way in English, a most appropriate name. Our second speaker was Pastor Buddy Hayes from Thorsby, Alabama. Brother Buddy has been our dear friend for over 40 years and he encouraged Bob so much with his presence.

How we thank the Lord for our special visitors from the United States—a group from the First Baptist Church in Loganville, Georgia, along with Pastor Billy Abrams from Cedar Grove Baptist Church in Leeds, Alabama and two ladies from the church. The Lord knows just what we need and when we need it. This group swept, mopped, cleaned windows, and on this dedication day they helped to serve 3000 people with only 1500 plates. **BUT WE DID IT** (another miracle), and when it was all over we all sat down and had a good laugh.

However, it wasn't so funny when it was happening! I was almost in panic when I saw three thousand people lined up for food. Just as Jesus did with the loaves and the fishes, He did it again with the chicken and rice.

How we ever had enough to feed every person is beyond my wildest imagination, but it happened. As far as I know, not one person left without something to eat. At number 1500, when we ran out of paper plates, we began serving food on top of loaf bread and putting this into their hands. So many of us were working and getting in each other's way; food was spilled on the floor, and that made it nice for slipping and sliding.

At the time, it was **CHAOS,** but all of this has turned into **beautiful, beautiful memories** of God's blessings and His provisions.

The Bible Institute opened on May 5, 2003 in the tabernacle with 50 young men anxious to study God's Word! God had given Bob the desires of his heart.

HOW CAN WE EVER THANK HIM ENOUGH FOR ALL THESE BEAUTIFUL MEMORIES OF HIS MARVELOUS WORKS AND ALLOWING BOB AND JOAN TYSON TO BE A PART OF ALL OF THIS....

48. The Prodigal Son Comes Home

"A Trophy of Grace"

For many years, we were known as "the Family Serving the Lord Together". That title ended when our oldest son, Philip, left the radio ministry that God had allowed him to build when he was only 21 years old. Five powerful radio stations beaming out the Gospel eighteen hours a day, seven days a week. The headaches came, then the mini strokes as I told about in an earlier chapter. The doctors at Emory Hospital in Atlanta, Georgia, gave him the medicine and the needles to inject himself when the headaches came. If not, he could have suffered a massive stroke.

December 3, 1997, Philip resigned from Good Samaritan Missions. Only a parent who has gone through an ordeal such as this could ever understand the pain. God had given us Felipe, as he is called, after 15 years of marriage. Bob had laid his hands on my stomach and dedicated him to the Lord, even named him, when he was still in my womb. There were no sonograms back then to tell if the baby was a boy or girl, but Bob just knew he would be a boy.

As a little boy growing up on the mission field, Philip was always curious, asking questions, making friends, and speaking Spanish like a Latin. As a young man, he was involved in almost every phase of the ministry.

The old Enemy, the devil, knew what he was doing. He wasn't after someone who had never done anything for the Lord, who wasn't interested in spiritual things. He was after a promising young man, who could easily follow in his dad's footsteps and carry on the ministry one day. He was after my son, and it didn't seem there was anything I could do.

Then it happened. Philip left us. I tried to give him counseling in the beginning. Philip had never been in the world. He had hardly ever dated anyone before he met his wife. He was pure and innocent. I don't think he ever intended to stray. I think he just wanted to get away from the pressures. That is the way the devil works—it comes a little at a time until an immunity is built up and nothing seems wrong.

Now and then Philip would call me. He was miserable. He hated his life. He would cry over the telephone. I begged him to make things right with the Lord. "What should I do?" he would say. And, of course, I told him the first thing he needed to do was to ask the Lord to forgive him, make a turn-around in his life, and then ask our pastors to forgive him, pastors who had loved him as a son and a brother and whom he had disappointed so much. He would not listen to me telling him to ask pastors to forgive him. "I have not done anything to them", he would say.

Then one day the call came. "Mom", he said. "I knew in my heart that if I did not find peace that I would kill myself. It was then that I fell on my knees and I asked God to forgive me. Would you ask Stevie to let me have a spot on the radio? I want to talk to everyone that I have wronged and disappointed". This was in 2003—over five years living in the hog pens of this world.

Thousands had been praying for Philip because those who knew him loved him and they knew how we, his parents, were suffering. And you, who have experienced this, know that feeling when your son or your daughter comes back "home". We were as the father who was watching afar off and saw his son coming. The father didn´t wait for the son to reach him; he ran to his son. **"Bring forth the best robe, and put it on him; and put a ring on his hand, and shoes on his feet"**.

That's what I wanted to do. My son was home. And that's how our heavenly Father feels when His children come home.

A date was planned for Philip to speak on the radio. It was announced everyday for a week that he would be speaking on a certain night.

Everyone gathered by their radios. He had just begun to speak when the electricity went out, and so went the radio. One of our pastors said he hurried to turn on his car radio to hear him speak.

We had to wait until the next night to hear him tell his story. He told of the life he had been living. He told how he could not go on without peace from God in his heart, and he told of how he had asked God to forgive him. He asked his mom and dad to forgive him. Then he did something that confirmed all he had been saying. He asked the pastors to forgive him, something he had told me he would never do because he had not sinned against them. But he came to the point where he humbled himself and asked forgiveness, not only from the Lord, but also from everyone he had wronged.

In 2004, he went before the Board of Directors of the Good Samaritan Baptist Missions and he asked forgiveness from them. There were board members who wept openly. They gave him a year of restoration before accepting him again on the Board of Good Samaritan Baptist Missions in 2005.

Philip returned to serve with a maturity and passion that he did not have before. I witnessed a deep love and a caring for every phase of the ministry, and it is amazing how God has blessed him in everything he does. I see more humbleness and a zeal to help everyone in any way he can.

Now, with Bob's health being so bad, and the responsibilities that I have, how could I handle all of this without the help of both my sons. I now have grandchildren who love this ministry and once again, we are a family working together for the Lord. This is our life; the purpose for our existence.

I realize there may be someone reading this book who finds it hard to forgive the prodigal son, just as the older brother in Luke 15—but if it should ever happen to you, as it did to Bob and me, then you will find it a lot easier in your heart to have compassion and forgiveness for others. To those who may have a wayward son or daughter, never give up! Prayer can move mountains. It did for us.

49. Walking Through The Valley Of The Shadow Of Death

"Yea, though I walk through the valley of the shadow of death, I will fear no evil: for thou art with me, thy rod and thy staff they comfort me". Psalm 23:4

I had felt tired all week but thought it was due to all the activities that had been going on, including the anniversary of our high school and attending to a group the week before. Stevie even called the doctor to come to the mission to see me. The doctor gave orders for me to go home and get some needed rest. However, I did not want to miss the last night of the anniversary program. As I climbed the steps to the high school, I began to feel very nauseated and dizzy. I made it to the bathroom and that's when I saw the blood. I went to the porch and sat down, hoping and praying it would just go away. But it didn't go away.

The time I spent in the doctor's office in San Marcos was to no avail. By this time, I think the whole town knew that I was seriously ill. Someone had called both Philip and Stevie in Tegucigalpa and the phone in the little clinic was ringing off the hook. "Get our mom to Tegucigalpa", they insisted.

The clinic inside and out was filled with people. We had three of our grandchildren with us and also Bob, who we could not leave alone. When we got in the van to leave from the clinic, I asked someone to pray and little Michael said, "I will pray, Grandma", and such a prayer I have never heard, coming from the mouth and heart of one so little. He said later that he never worried about me again because he had asked Jesus to help me.

Mario was driving the van as we left out for the long three and a half hour trip to a hospital in Tegucigalpa. The doctor had given me a pan to vomit the blood in. I laid down on the front seat of the van with my face in front of the air-conditioner because I was so nauseated. Before we reached Choluteca, I was so sick, perspiration was dripping off my face, yet my whole body was cold. I had to stop by the side of the road to use the bathroom and it was pure blood. "Mario, I don't think I am going to make it". I cannot believe that I said that so calmly. Stephany began to cry and said that I was going to make it. Mario had a choice of stopping at the general hospital in Choluteca, which would be impossible to describe the condition of this hospital, or to take me on to Tegucigalpa, another two hours away. He made the decision to keep going.

Meanwhile Stevie and Philip continued calling. "Where are you?" "Drive faster!", they would say. I can remember at one time Mario saying, "I have the gas pedal all the way". There are so many check points here where the police stop you to check your papers but Mario would only slow down, roll down the window and say, "I have someone gravely ill in my car" and keep going.

From the time we left home, I began to not only pray but I would repeat Bible verses in my mind and then I would sing all the hymns that I knew by memory – saying to myself that if the Lord let me live, I would learn more Bible verses.

As I think back on this now, I cannot remember one time that I was afraid to die, and yes, I felt like I would probably not make it. It seems strange to me now and I think, "Why was I not afraid? No one wants to die". I believe there is *grace* for every need. God gave me grace that night lying on the front seat of that van, vomiting blood from my mouth and blood coming from my bowels. He gave me the assurance that the Lord never leaves us nor forsakes us and whatever His will is, He will keep us in perfect peace.

About thirty minutes out of Tegucigalpa, Philip and Stevie were both out looking for our van. Philip had gotten an ambulance (our van was much better), and Stevie was in a truck with the doctor. He was going so fast that he completely passed us without seeing us.

The ambulance brought me on to the hospital where they literally tore my clothes off, trying to take blood tests, etc., to determine what type blood I had. Never knowing this before, I discovered I had A Negative blood, a very rare type here. The hospital had very little of this blood and so immediately the task began of trying to find A Negative blood.

When word got out that I needed blood, through the radio and word of mouth, there were four people from far back in Nicaragua who came all the way to Tegucigalpa to give me blood. Out of an organization as big as we have in Honduras, only our librarian in the high school had this type blood, also the brother of one of our teachers. Other people gave different types of blood to repay the hospital for the blood they had given me.

I was told later that the doctors had very little hope for me because I had lost so much blood but several days and 8 pints of blood and plasma later, I was able to return home

The doctors in Tegucigalpa said that my problem was caused by a blood thinner that I was taking and advised me not to take this medicine again.

More bad news is on the way....

50. "Boast Not Thyself Of Tomorrow"

In the months after my illness, I felt great and immediately went back to work. We returned to the states for Christmas of 2004 and were excited about returning to Honduras. Our plans were made; suitcases were packed, but God had other plans.

Visiting our family doctor with Bob and Stephany, who had colds, I mentioned to him about the problems I had last August in Honduras with my stomach. Nothing would do but for me to have this checked out before returning to Honduras. Although I did not want to have this done, and even arguing with him a little and assuring him that I was fine and had never felt better in my life, I finally gave in to have these tests.

After testings by three specialists, a tumor was found in the wall of my stomach. This, no doubt, the doctors said, is what caused the hemorrhage in my stomach.

I was sent to a surgeon at Piedmont Hospital in Atlanta and the picture painted to me was bleak. He showed us the picture on the computer screen, a shadow that looked like it covered three fourths of my stomach. He explained that most of my stomach would have to be removed, along with my spleen and possibly my gallbladder—that I would only be able to eat two or three tablespoons of food every two hours for the rest of my life, and on and on. Stephany and Stevie were both with me and once again Stephany began to cry. I will never forget Dr. Barnett putting his arms around Stephany and consoling her, telling her not to worry that he was going to take care of me.

"Do you believe in prayer?" I asked the doctor. "I believe in the power of prayer," he replied with a smile.

Our Christian family in Honduras, Nicaragua, Costa Rica, Mexico, Puerto Rico, and here in the United States began to fast and pray. On March 11, 2005, as I was rolled into the operating room, there were thousands on their knees praying me though this operation. They had been opening the church doors at 4:00 a.m. for people to come in and pray. There were designated places to pray all during the time of my operation, which included all the high school and grammar school children.

The hospital called the morning of my surgery and told me I could come in earlier because they had a cancellation.

"I would like to cooperate with you", I said, "but there are thousands of people in Central America who will be on their knees at the exact time I will be going into surgery, and I do not want to go in early".

"I don't blame you a bit", she replied. "I wouldn't come in early either".

I knew people were praying because I had a peace which passeth all understanding, a peace that is indescribable, which I told to the doctor and nurses.

The waiting room at Piedmont Hospital was also filled with pastors and friends.

The doctor himself was surprised when he found the tumor, which he said was about the size of a plum. He was able to remove this, clean all around it, and didn't have to remove anything else except for about 30% of my stomach.

He later sent me to an Oncologist who took my papers to the receptionist, looked at me and said, **"CURED, CASE CLOSED"**. No further need for any kind of treatment. The Oncologist and Dr. Barnett told me that this type of tumor is very dangerous because there are hardly any symptoms until the tumor is so large that sometimes they can't even operate. They also said they were sure the hemorrhage in Honduras had come from this tumor, which was a blessing in disguise.

I think about how close we came to returning to Honduras without seeing a doctor, and how I told Dr. Boss of my problem when we were only there to take care of Bob and Stephany, not for me. I think of Dr. Boss´ insistence that I see a specialist and how I even argued a little with him. The specialist even sent me to another specialist to be 100% sure, and he told me then that it was probably cancer.

"BOAST NOT THYSELF OF TOMORROW; FOR THOU KNOWEST NOT WHAT A DAY MAY BRING FORTH." Proverbs 27:1

I have always tried to say, "I will do this or that, **IF IT IS GOD´S WILL**". We were so sure that it was God's will to return to Honduras to be there for the new year when all the schools opened again, for all the meetings we had planned with the directors of the different ministries, etc., but God had other plans. He has a purpose for everything that happens to His children.

I had a call from our high school principal, and she said that nothing had affected our mission in Honduras as my sickness and operation had done--teachers, office workers, pastors, students and children, had been brought together in a way that she could not even describe. They were all on their knees at 1:00 p.m. (11:00 a.m. US time) when I was rolled into the operating room.

It was after 5:00 p.m. when the call came from the US that everything was ok, and this was put over the loud speaker at the school where everyone was waiting. Shouts and screams of rejoicing went up everywhere and teachers were crying and thanking the Lord. The principal also said that as in every organization there are people who are not very appreciative, or who do not think about the sacrifice that a missionary makes, but this had brought everyone together in a way that was nothing short of a miracle.

I received a call from our national director in Nicaragua, who told me that over one hundred churches in Nicaragua opened their doors for people to come in and pray at 1:00 p.m., on March 11, and that hearing the news of how God had performed this miracle, had caused everyone to give thanks and honor and glory to the Lord.

God used so many people in my life during this time—a caring friend and family doctor, Dr. Larry Boss, from Villa Rica, Georgia, who has been our family doctor for years. He told me that in his forty years of practicing medicine, he had never seen a case just like mine. God used the doctors who told me they were almost 100% sure it was cancer and sent me to a wonderful and caring surgeon in Atlanta. He used the nurses who took care of me and who allowed Stephany to stay in the room with me throughout the time I was hospitalized, even though she was under age.

As we were checking out of the hospital, one of the nurses commented that we were going to be missed because we had brought excitement to the hospital. She said that never had they had a patient who had as many visitors as I did. I believe the nurses really enjoyed seeing the happiness in the faces of all those people who came to see me, giving praises to the Lord.

And most of all, God used His people who would not give up—they prayed, they fasted, they begged God to spare my life—and **He did.**

When we visited Dr. Barnett for the last time on April the 13th, I asked him when I would be able to go home. "When do you want to go home?" He asked. I said, "April the 17th", which was only four days away.

He looked at me with a big smile and said, **"Go back and save more souls in Honduras!"**

51. Missionary Journeys

2005 and 2006 were very busy years. Enrollments in our combined schools were reaching close to 2000 students. The Bible Institute was graduating young men who had a desire to go into new areas of Honduras and Nicaragua to win souls and establish churches and always they wanted me to come when there was a church dedication or just to come and see what God was doing.

I never cease to be amazed at how God works. I had a desire to visit these places but it would be overnight trips and I needed another lady to go with me. The Lord sent me the best—a young lady from the Lupton Drive Baptist Church in Chattanooga, Tennessee—Kathy Little, who came down to teach English in our high school for a few months.

Little did we realize what God had in store for us on Saturday, March 11, 2006, when we left at 6:00 am to visit our newest work in San Luis, Santa Barbara, Honduras. Ten hours later, we arrived in this little mountain town where we were given the royal treatment. Passing through towns and villages that I had only read about occasionally in the newspaper, we finally arrived to meet some of the sweetest people that I have ever met in Honduras.

Edwin and Leyda Miranda had gone to this place as missionaries after a former Science teacher in our high school had moved there to take care of her elderly mother. God burdened her heart for her pueblo and she contacted us, asking for a preacher. Brother Edwin said, **"I will go."** Souls had been saved and a Baptist church raised up in this town. They were begging me to come and see what God was doing in this place.

Everyone was inviting us to visit their homes and everywhere we went they wanted to serve us food. We walked to the open-air services that night and on Sunday morning, we were fed fried beans, fresh cream (from the cow), and tortillas at the Judge's house. The wife of the Judge had recently been saved and she treated us as if we were royalty.

After service on Sunday morning, our group slit up for lunch because more than one wanted us to eat with them. A little after 1:00 p.m., we continued on our missionary journey to a place further on in the mountains where we had received another "Macedonian" call.

We thought it would take about 2 and 1/2 hours but five hours later we were driving on **"trails"** and had no idea where we were. Edwin went with us but he had only been to this place one time; it was at night and his memory failed him when we came to all the crossroads, or trails I might say. Thank the Lord for our jeep!

We stopped and asked a man on the side of the road if we were on the right road to La Capuca, but even Mario, our driver, got tongue tied on this one and looked at me with a face of dismay and asked ME, OF ALL PEOPLE, how to pronounce the name of where we were going…just as if I KNEW. This turned out to be very funny…a Honduran asking ME HOW TO PRONOUNCE A WORD IN SPANISH!

Anyway, the man told us to keep going straight and we did, only the little road was far from straight. It was after 7:00 p.m., and very dark, when we reached the house of Brother Omar, sitting in the middle of a huge coffee plantation. The experiences we had in La Capuca will live with me for the rest of my life.

The next morning, we could see exactly where we were. What a beautiful place we were in! We were surrounded by large coffee plantations and it was absolutely gorgeous; beautiful, beautiful flowers growing everywhere and the tallest trees I have ever seen in my life.

Brother Omar, owner of the property, talked to me the next morning and made his offer to me. "If you will send us a preacher, I will give the mission the deed to the church that I built with my own money and also will give land for a pastorium", he said.

I immediately gave him my answer. "We are not interested in more property and land for the mission," I told him. "God has to touch a preacher's heart to come here. It is not up to us to send someone."

He later told the pastors that had this been another mission he was sure they would have accepted the land in a minute and that he admired me for my honesty and sincerity with him. I also told him that this had to be of the Lord; 15 hours away in the mountains of Honduras, no doctors, no stores to buy groceries, just living off the land. A preacher would have to have a definite call from God just as Bob Tyson received way back in 1964.

Well, later one of our preachers did volunteer to go to La Capuca. While moving them there in the large truck of the mission, Mario said he had to stop and console the wife who had no idea where they were going. Thank God for national preachers who are willing to go at anytime and anywhere to preach the Gospel of Jesus Christ.

And, as for Edwin and his wife in San Luis, it has been almost four years since our first visit to the new work there. Stephany and I went back two years ago, and I have just been invited to attend the 6th grade graduation of their Christian school. The little church has thrived and there is now a Christian kindergarten through sixth grades. Land is very expensive here because of the coffee plantations, but they are trusting the Lord to help them buy land.

There were many more missionary journeys for Kathy and me. When we get together now, we reminisce over these past experiences that God has engraved in our minds and hearts.

There is one other trip that brought so much joy to us and I just want to highlight some of this journey to Vallecillo, Honduras.

It all began with Brother Abel Arias who came to our Bible Institute to study from Vallecillo and then returned after graduation to raise up a work in his village.

I will never forget the first day that Brother Abel came to the Institute. As always, I would go out and talk to the students about keeping the tabernacle clean, how Brother Bob always wanted God's property to be the cleanest and most well kept in the town. As I finished my little speech, Brother Abel raised his hand and asked if he could say something.

"Sister Joan,", he said. "We know that your customs are different than our customs. When we clear our throats and have to spit, we spit on the floor. Do we spit on the floor here or just where do we spit?"

I could not believe what I was hearing. I could see that the older students were trying hard to keep from laughing. As I looked around the beautiful auditorium of the tabernacle, the beautiful white benches and tile floor, I quietly asked the others, "Is Brother Abel asking me if you all can spit on this floor?" When I said this, everyone began to laugh. But Brother Abel was sincere; the most humble, and sincere student we had.

Now, he had graduated and we were invited to his church—another long, missionary journey. Kathy went with me and this time Stephany and Philip, Jr., went along.

What a beautiful, beautiful place back in the mountains about 2 and 1/2 hours the other side of Tegucigalpa. I have never heard singing that beautiful in Honduras. Brother Abel and his family (he had 13 children) walked some three hours to get to church and I suppose this is where they learned to sing—harmonizing on the trails. They were meeting in a small house on the side of the mountain. I could just imagine a pretty little church built there.

After service we were taken to another little house beside the house where we were meeting, and there the women from the church had cooked for us over open fire. Back then, Stephany was still a little "picky" with what she ate; Kathy was a LOT "picky," and this was something new for Philip, Jr. Stephany decided she would just go to the car while we ate, and Philip decided he would accompany her. Kathy had not said a word.

"Go on to the car," I said. "Forget about these ladies standing here on this dirt floor over open fire, cooking a meal for us that they would not have the blessing of eating themselves."

I looked around at the little table—chicken broth, boiled chicken on a separate plate, some boiled potatoes, sweet potatoes, and patasta. Mario and I sat down, and so did Kathy, Stephany and Philip, Jr. No one said a word—we just started filling our plates. The people were standing around to see if we liked the food. Stephany was the first to remark, "this is really good," and we all ate and the people smiled.

These people made me feel like I was about an inch tall when I compared my own life and sacrifice for the Lord to the love, faith and sacrifice that they have for the Lord and His work. How many times have I walked three to four hours to go to a church service? How many times have I served others a meal that I could not afford to eat myself?

Thank the Lord for the Philadelphia Baptist Church in Calhoun, Georgia. They wanted to do something in honor of two of their older members, Brother A.D. and Bea Bowman. They sent money for construction of a beautiful church in Vallecillo. We had the great privilege of going back there for the dedication of the new building on September 2, 2007. Jim Smith from North Point Baptist Church in Carrollton, Georgia went with us for this precious service.

We again were served with a delicious meal—a little different this time. The meat was so tender you could cut it with a fork. As Stephany was enjoying the delicious meat, she kept asking, "What kind of meat is this?", to which I hastily replied, "Just eat, Stephany, and don't ask any questions." I was suspicious that it was "cow tongue" but I kept remembering my first sermon about not eating the food when we ate on the little porch more than two years before.

There are so many more missionary stories that I have stored up in my memory but time nor space permits me to share these with you now.

I thank God for His many, many marvelous works that He has blessed me to have a part in and for allowing me to still be able to remember.

And I thank the Lord for Kathy Little, who was always ready to go with me, no matter where we were going, and sitting down at a table to eat "only the Lord knows what," **but she ate,** and she kept that sweet smile that touched the heart of everyone who met her.

52. "Grace Annex" Grammar School Extension

In 1989, we started the grammar school in an old run-down cantina with 180 students, and in 1999 the Lord allowed us to build a beautiful grammar school building. In 2006 our enrollment had grown to over 600. ABSOLUTELY no more room! We had two shifts from 7:00 am until 7:00 pm.

The time had come that I must make a decision. Do I say **"enough,"** or do I step out by faith and have more rooms built to our grammar school?

The principal had told me at the beginning of the year that the classrooms were too full, yet we kept sponsoring more children because I didn't have the heart to turn them away. I always think that this may be the child that God is going to use one day to be a preacher or a missionary, and how can we turn him away.

I knew in my heart what Bob would have done. He would have told me to go forward, but I needed to hear these words come from his mouth. Sadly to say, this time he couldn't help me. His memory was getting worse. Thank the Lord He still remembered his family, and on more than one occasion I would ask him, "What do you think I should do?" or "Should I do this or that?" and he would answer me—but this time he just stared into space. "God, please help me to make the right decision," I prayed.

In October 2006, I sent out a newsletter telling about this need. "The cost of this annex to our grammar school, which will include a library and new computer lab, is going to be approximately $100,000.00."

Before sending the 2006 newsletter to the printers, I added a HUGE postscript and these were my words.

> "I had an opportunity to speak at the MLC Heart and Home Ministries Retreat in Gatlinburg, Tennessee, headed up by my wonderful friend, Mary Lynn Crider. Mary Lynn had asked me about our needs and I told her about the need for more space in our grammar school. She shared this with the ladies present for this conference. She asked for a chair to put at the edge of the platform, and asked me to sit down—and as I sat there, 400 ladies passed by and laid $35,000 at my feet."

I don't think there was a dry eye in the building. **I was in a state of shock.** This was only the beginning. They continued to give until they gave every cent that was needed.

In April 2007, the beautiful **"Grace Annex"** was dedicated to the Lord. It was named **"Grace"** in memory of Mary Lynn's mother, Grace, who was a blessing to everyone who knew her. She was truly a special lady, filled with grace and love. She collected doves so we thought it was fitting to add some doves to the top of the annex. Our only problem was that we could not find doves anywhere. Oscar, the builder, fearing that we would not be able to find any doves to mount on top, had doves carved into every door of the new building—**Absolutely beautiful!**

And then, we found a man in the capital who made huge doves for us which were mounted on the top of the building. (This was another unbelievable sight—witnessing about 15 men trying to hoist these huge doves by rope onto the top of the building.)

The dedication was attended by a group of ladies from the MLC retreat, including Jane Keel and Sandy Payton, precious friends who provided special music for us all week. In attendance was a Colonel from the military, the Mayor of the large city of Choluteca, and also some business people from town. The school children put on a beautiful drama about the resurrection of our Lord.

At the end of the dedication, several of the children were holding live doves, which they turned loose—a very beautiful and touching ceremony.

The following Sunday morning, a businessman came forward in church to openly profess his faith in Christ. In his testimony he told of being at the dedication service and how the Lord touched his heart when the children were putting on the drama of the resurrection. **We never, never know how the Lord is going to work!**

Tommy and Mary Lynn, along with all the ladies of the MLC retreat, have continued to be a blessing to this work, and especially to me. They have held conferences, which has been a blessing to hundreds of pastors and their wives. The MLC ladies gave money for a new church building and feeding kitchen in the village of Papalon. They came when the church was meeting under a tree; they saw the need, and they gave. On one occasion they gave $10,000 to finish a cafeteria in our high school. After visiting us and staying at the mission center, they saw the need for new bathrooms and floor in our mission center, and they did something about it. They have sponsored many, many little children. At the present time, they are working on another project.

I thank God for the people that He has brought into our lives; people that we didn't even know, and some we still do not know, but He has used these wonderful people to show us that there is **ABSOLUTELY NOTHING IMPOSSIBLE FOR GOD.**

What if I had said, "No, it is too much. It is better to stay where we are and not sponsor any more children; it is too much money"? Just think what I would have missed, and just think of the hundreds of little children who would have missed out on their **"Opportunity of a Lifetime."**

Thank you, Lord, for giving me the faith to go forward, and thank you Lord for Tommy and Mary Lynn and every person who gave to the **"Grace Annex"** project.

53. Bob's Health

July 12, 2002—We were seeing a group off from the airport in Tegucigalpa when Bob complained of a severe pain on the side of his neck. Later in the afternoon, this same thing happened again except the pain was worse—his kidneys were out of control for over an hour and he had a hard chill.

We immediately began preparations to take him to the states. While Stevie was checking him in at the airport on Monday morning, he passed out at the American Airlines counter with what we later learned was a seizure. The Airlines would not allow him to fly until orders were given by a doctor.

At last, after taking medicine, he was given permission to fly and was taken directly from the Atlanta airport to the Villa Rica Hospital where he spent the next five days. He suffered another seizure within four hours after being discharged and was transported back to the hospital where he spent four days in Intensive Care and more time in the hospital.

It would be several weeks before we would be able to return to Honduras. This latest illness had caused Bob to lose more of his precious memories and it was heartbreaking for me. We used to sit on the front porch and I would talk to him about all the **marvelous works** God had done in our lives, the miracles He had performed, and Bob's eyes would well up with tears. He understood what I was saying, and then he would forget.

August 10, 2003—Bob turned 69 years old. On Saturday, the 9th, all our pastors and their wives came from far and near to the tabernacle to celebrate his birthday. One by one, they stood and thanked him for obeying God's call and bringing the Gospel to them.

For the next couple of years, Bob remained about the same. He had his good days and bad days—days that his mind was more alert and days that he had a lot of problems.

June 6, 2006—Bob suffered another seizure. We immediately called the doctor who came to the house and gave him a shot. Later he sent a male nurse to spend the night and watch him.

The next morning we took Bob to the Medical Center in Tegucigalpa, a good hospital which had recently been built. When the Neurologists examined Bob, the first thing they told us was that he did not have Alzheimers. After further examinations, including a spinal tap, they told us he had "water on the brain" and needed surgery immediately. They would put in a shunt to keep the water drained. They assured us that without complications Bob's memory could be restored.

In one week after surgery, we were able to bring him home from the hospital, and there was a great improvement in his memory and in his speech. He talked with Stephany and me better and more than he had in several years. Stevie filmed his dad talking about his childhood, his dad's ministry, and his own ministry in Nicaragua and Honduras. Bob's last words to Stevie before the battery ran out on the camera, "If I don't see you anymore here, I will see you up yonder. **Keep on the firing line**," (the name of an old hymn we used to sing in church years ago).

Shortly thereafter, Bob became very restless, slurring his words, and not able to remember. We rushed him back to the hospital and they told us they needed to remove the shunt and replace it with another. The shunt was malfunctioning.

Another operation followed and this time more problems—there was bleeding on the brain. I did not leave the hospital for days. At last, on a Friday I decided to come back to our office in San Marcos de Colón, sign checks or do whatever I needed to do.

While I was in San Marcos, Bob had another seizure. This time he swallowed his tongue, and went into a coma. The doctors did not know how long he had gone without breathing. He was immediately put on a breathing machine and this is the condition in which I found him when I returned from San Marcos. I knew nothing about this until I returned late that afternoon. He was in Intensive Care with a breathing tube down his throat. They had not called me, deciding it would be better to wait until I returned.

For days, Bob was like a dead person. His whole body swelled and he was not breathing at all on his own. The hospital gave me a room next to ICU. Every day there were large groups of people coming to the hospital; one day there were 70 people in the waiting room and the halls. No one wanted me to be alone, but my body was crying out for rest. I did not want to offend anyone so I stayed until the last one left and got up when the first ones came in the mornings.

On a Sunday night, two Neurosurgeons came to my room and talked with Philip, Stevie and me. We had to make a decision. Did we want him to continue indefinitely on the breathing machine? His lungs were filling up and his body was swollen. What they wanted to do was a tracheotomy because he was not breathing on his own and this would keep him alive. However, there was no assurance that he would not remain in a vegetable state for the rest of his life.

To take him off the breathing machine would mean sudden death unless God intervened, because he was only breathing 10% on his own.

Philip, Stevie, and I knew that Bob would never want to live like this. We knelt by the bedside and prayed, but my prayer to God was that we would not have to make this decision—that He would intervene. However, we gave the authorization to take him off the machine, praying that God's will be done. This was to take place at 8:00 the next morning.

About 6:00 a.m. the next morning, I was awakened by a nurse who told me I was needed in ICU. I thought the worse. However, when I walked through the door, the ICU nurse said, "Look at your husband!" Bob was lying there, with his eyes open, looking around. They had not taken him off the breathing machine but he was breathing 100% on his own. I took his hand and asked if he knew me. **He squeezed my hand**!

A few minutes later, the doctor came to my room and told me that they were removing the tube immediately. When I asked about his lungs, because just a few hours before, he was swelling from so much liquid build-up, the doctor simply said, "His lungs are clear." By 8:00 a.m., the breathing tube was removed, and that afternoon, he was moved to a private room.

Later when I told the doctor that he was a good doctor, he made the statement, "Do not thank me; this came from a higher power." A nurse heard this and told me later that this doctor had **never** given credit to God for anything.

Upon the advice of the doctors, we rented an apartment near the hospital as Bob needed to have special care for the next two or three months. This small apartment looked like a mini-hospital with nurses and doctors coming from the hospital to care for Bob. The hospital bill was enormous and our insurance did not cover medical care outside of the United States. It was cheaper for us to continue his treatment in an apartment outside the hospital. We thank the Lord for the many friends and family that helped us financially during this time.

In two months we were back at home with the assurance from the doctors that Bob would fully recuperate in time. He had to learn to walk again and had to be spoon fed for several weeks. His speech was still very slurred, but he enjoyed lying in bed and listening to hymns over the radio. He would try to sing and we rejoiced.

No one could believe that Bob had gone through so much and was still with us. God heard the prayers of His people and was leaving Bob with us for a while longer.

54. Showers Of Blessings

In the years 2004 to 2007, the blessings God shed upon this mission are too numerous to mention.

Bob Tyson was not able to represent the mission in the United States and raise money for the many projects and also get help for the children, but that was no problem for God. He sent the churches to us.

Group after group, sometimes seven and eight back-to-back groups, came and brought **blessings—and blessings in abundance.** Groups rode on the back of trucks giving out thousands and thousands of food bags to the poor; clothes were given to the needy—hundreds of children were sponsored and money was given for projects. It caused all of us to give thanks to our Heavenly Father for the way He was providing for His people.

Not only physical blessings were brought to us, but spiritual blessings as well. Bob Tyson could no longer teach the pastors but the Lord took care of that also. Men of God such as Dr. Guy Altizer, Dr. Billy Martin, Missionary Richard Comer, and others, held Bible conferences for our national pastors that brought a revival to everyone who attended. Conferences on the home and marriage by Rev. Tommy Crider and Mary Lynn, Dr. Altizer and his wife, a group from the Grace Baptist Church in Powder Springs, Georgia, and others, touched the lives of our pastors and their wives.

There were many new churches raised up during this time, and hundreds saved and baptized.

Oscar Vallejo, one of our pastors, and also the one who heads up all our construction projects in Honduras, was kept busy during this period of time finishing one project and going to another. When Oscar received the Lord, he was the main builder for a very large religious organization. Upon receiving the Lord and being called to preach, he was told to make a choice––give up this new "religion" and he would have work for as long as he wanted—or continue as a Gospel believer, and he would lose his job. He tells how he sadly walked away that day wondering what would happen with such a large family to feed.

He came to our Bible Institute by faith and has not been without work since that time. In fact, when he left his other job, he only had a bicycle for transportation, now he has a nice truck. I wonder when we are so blessed with offerings to build churches, pastoriums, Feed the Hungry kitchens, etc., if it is God answering the prayers of the people in the churches or if he is taking care of Oscar. I already know the answer. God is taking care of ALL His children.

During this time, the old Mission center in Condega was completely re-constructed. Hardly anything had been done to this building since the war.

I was thinking that we only needed to put on a roof and patch up a few things. However, when they started taking off the roof, the building almost fell in.

I sent Philip to see what we needed to do because he has always had an eye and knowledge for building like his dad. The first time I went to see this "re-construction," I could only stare in amazement. There was nothing there but a floor and one wall. We ended up practically rebuilding the complete mission center, plus eight new rooms were built for our schools and two rooms for the offices. This is the most beautiful place in town! Philip did a wonderful job choosing the style, tile, colors, etc. This is a testimony for the **"GOSPEL BELIEVERS."**

Once again, I asked the Lord to please help me. I never thought we would have to spend so much money. With the offerings that had been received for this project, we still needed $40,000.00.

One day, while eating lunch, I received a phone call from our office in the states, "Are you sitting down?" Terri asked me. I just knew something bad had happened. "No," she said. "Nothing bad has happened. You just got a check from a couple in California for the rebuilding of the mission center in Condega in the amount of $40,000.00." This was the exact amount we needed to finish the construction. As far as I knew, I had never met these people. The lady who called told Terri that her heart was touched when she read my letter; she told her husband that she would like to help, but that she didn´t know how much to send. He asked her how much I needed and when she told him the amount, he said, **"Send it All."**

And so there stands a beautiful Mission Center and Christian school building in Condega, Nicaragua—the same place where we once were called **"hogs"** some 38 years ago.

I wrote a letter to these dear people in California thanking them for this very generous offering, and then wrote another letter inviting them to come to the dedication, but I never heard a word. Someone told me, **"Maybe angels don´t write letters."**

55. "Home-Going" Of Bob Tyson

"And I heard a voice from heaven saying unto me, Write, Blessed are the dead which die in the Lord from henceforth: Yea, saith the Spirit, that they may rest from their labors; and their works do follow them." —Revelation 14:13

We saw daily improvements in Bob's health after his surgery. He even went to church with us in the tabernacle. "What a beautiful building," he said. "But the benches are too hard." He would have good days and bad days, mostly with a terrible pain in his neck, which some said could have been caused by the position they kept him in for such a long time during the surgeries. He also lost a lot of weight, even though his appetite was good.

He was surrounded by people who loved him—me, his grandchildren, Luz, our housekeeper, and a practical nurse who took care of him in the daytime and a sitter at night. He was never alone. I thank the Lord that he was well cared for.

I moved my office to our home so that I could be with him. We put a small cot in my office and he could lie there and watch me while I worked. Many times he would walk over to my desk to see if he could help me. I cherish those memories. Sometimes we would sit in the swing on the porch and I would talk to him about his life and how the Lord had used him in Central America. I would go over his calling to preach and his calling to be a missionary. He would listen intently. Sometimes the tears would come; other times he would tell me he could not remember.

Dr. Larry Boss, our family doctor, came to see him, which was a blessing to Bob and to all of our family. I will never forget the prayer that Dr. Boss prayed for Bob before he left for the United States.

Saturday night, the 19th of May, was the sitter's night off. Armando, who is one of the drivers for the mission and has worked for us for years, volunteered to sit with him. I was getting ready for bed and Stephany was on the phone talking to her dad, Philip, in Tegucigalpa, when she heard a noise. She looked through a small window in her room and could see Armando trying to lift Bob up off the floor. She ran immediately to see what had happened, and when she saw the large lump on the side of his head, she came running for me. I knelt beside him and asked Armando what had happened. He told me that Bob had tripped over a floor-fan, and hit his head on the hard tile.

Armando and I walked with him; he came back to lie down, and then said he had to use the bathroom. We walked with him to the bathroom, but when we got him back to the bed, he began to vomit. Shortly after that, he closed his eyes and didn't speak or move again. I realized then just how serious this was.

We had been in contact with Philip since the fall and so now I called him again and told him that he and Stevie needed to come. Both lived in the capital. We sent for the local doctor who stayed with us the rest of the night.

As soon as Philip came, he called the neurosurgeon in Tegucigalpa, who had operated on Bob, and explained to him what had happened. He was already in a state of coma—clear liquid had come from his nose, which we later learned was liquid from his brain caused by the severe injury to his head. His eyes were not dilated. The doctor said that the decision to bring him to Tegucigalpa, 3 ½ hours away, was ours, but he would not recommend it. Philip also called Dr. Boss in Villa Rica, Georgia, explaining everything to him. Dr. Boss asked him to check his eyes and his pulse. There was no movement of his eyes with light. It seemed that his body had shut down. So we waited, and the local doctor waited with us, doing all she could.

7:10 p.m., May 20---- I was standing close to the foot of his bed, when I heard him take a deep breath—he **exhaled** and he was **gone**. It reminded me of someone who comes into the house after working outside all day, sits down in his favorite chair, and breathes in and lets out a deep sigh of relief—**rest at last**. I think this is what happened to Bob. He was so tired, and when the Lord finally took him, he drew in a deep breath of relief; he let it out, and then he was gone. He went into that eternal rest, never to be tired anymore; never to hurt anymore. He was at rest from **"all his labors."**

Another thought came to my mind that night. Bob had traveled hundreds of thousands of miles all over the United States to raise money for the Lord's work, but he couldn't take one cent with him. He had built some of the most beautiful buildings in Central America, but he couldn't take one building with him. All that he could take with him when he drew his last breath was the fruit from his labors—souls that had been saved.

Sunday night church service was just about to end when someone called one of the deacons and said that Brother Bob had just passed away. The service immediately dismissed and within a few minutes, there were probably 200 people in the street, in our yard, and in the house.

I have never seen such an outpouring of love.

It took about four hours or more for the hearse (which was really a van) to come from Tegucigalpa. At about 4:00 a.m., we were trying to find a casket in the dimly lit funeral home. In fact, a flashlight had to be used in the room where the caskets were kept. His body was to be embalmed, which is very rare here, but we needed to have this done because of the time involved before burial.

At about 8:00 a.m., we were following behind the van trying to find the place where they told us we would have to go to have an autopsy performed. We had just learned that this was required to be able to take his body out of the country. The autopsy revealed, "Severe skull fracture caused by a fall."

All day long we went from one office to another, trying to get the necessary papers, and also a visit to the American Embassy for the red tape that was necessary there. The Lord had a wonderful businessman named Adan, a friend of Stevie's, who stayed with us all day and helped us to find the many offices where we had to go. Late in the day, we had to buy another casket because they told us the airlines required a certain kind of casket.

I will never forget when we were in the place where the autopsy was to be performed (just a little building out in the middle of a field). A taxi came up with a young girl and her father. It was evident something terrible had happened. Another daughter had just been found murdered, with over 70 stab wounds in her body. We could tell they were very poor. Stevie's wife, Scarleth, put her arms around this grieving sister and asked if they needed a casket. "We have no money to buy one," she cried. "My mother-in-law has one that she will not be using and I am sure she will be more than happy to give it to you," Scarleth told her. We had been told that the casket we had bought did not meet the requirements of the airline, making it necessary to buy another casket. And so, Bob's first casket went to good use.

While we were trying to get all the necessary paper work done in the capital, the people in San Marcos were planning his funeral. Hundreds of people waited for us to bring Bob back to the tabernacle for the "wake" on Monday night. We finally arrived after midnight. I could not believe all the people that had been waiting for hours. Tents were set up outside the tabernacle to feed the hundreds of people who came from out of town. Our family did not have to do anything—the people who loved him cooked the food, served the people, planned the funeral, directed the traffic, and did it while they shed tears for their beloved missionary. They had even had two services earlier that night.

The service started after we arrived at about 1:30 a.m., and lasted until 4:00 a.m. I finally went home at 4:30 a.m. and slept for about two hours. Many stayed all night and until the funeral the next day because they did not want him to be left alone (the same custom as it was when I was a young girl in the United States). The funeral was scheduled for 10:00 a.m.

The registration offices of births and deaths were on strike all over Honduras making it impossible to get a death certificate, which was necessary before we could export Bob's body. **God used all of this for His honor and glory.**

Philip knew people in very high positions in the Government of Honduras and they became involved in this. While Bob's funeral was going on, a proclamation was given that said, "The nationwide strike will be lifted for 30 minutes in order for a death certificate to be given to Rev. Bob Tyson."

In his death, he stopped a national strike, and when the American Embassy commented to Philip and me that they did not realize that Rev. Tyson was so well known all over Honduras, we commented that neither Bob nor we knew he was well known—he never received nor desired honor in his lifetime.

When we were at the airport to leave Honduras, three dignitaries representing the Government came to apologize to our family for the delay in getting his death certificate issued, and they stayed with our family until we boarded the plane.

The funeral in the United States was beautiful. Hundreds from many different states came to say goodbye to their missionary and to give us comfort. National pastors from every country where Bob had served came to the funeral. Maura came from Puerto Rico.

And so a great man of God was called home. But the work of God goes forward.

56. The Trials And Tragedies

"Beloved, think it not strange concerning the fiery trial which is to try you, as though some strange thing happened unto you." —I Peter 4:12

Had it not been for perfect peace from the Lord after Bob's passing, I could have never kept going, but the Lord did give me His perfect peace. I could get through the problems but it is hard for me to see others suffer. I want to fix the problem but things happened that could not be "fixed."

Not too long after Bob's death, Pastor Luis Ramirez, Pueblo Nuevo, Nicaragua, only 46 years old, had a stroke in his brain and died immediately, leaving a wife and four children. My heart went out to his wife and children, now left without a husband and a father. There is no Social Security or retirement for a pastor in these countries. How would they live? I thank the Lord that He has provided in the way that only He could do it.

In February 2007, one of our seniors, Erick, drowned in the river in San Marcos de Colón. This was a terrible time for our students. His body was taken to the high school and his funeral was held there.

On October 14, 2007, which was Stephany´s birthday, we experienced a terrible tragedy here at the boys´ dorm. One of our seniors drowned in the pond behind the boys' dorm. Jaime Diaz had just turned 19 and would have been the first in his family to graduate from high school. He had rededicated his life to the Lord just a few weeks earlier when Pastor Rodney Agan and a group from North Point Baptist Church in Carrollton, Georgia were here for a youth conference. He was baptized on Tuesday night before he drowned on Sunday morning. We had put a picture in one of our newsletters about this conference, and the picture showed Jaime as he was praying and re-dedicating his life to the Lord.

We will never know what Jaime was thinking when he jumped into the pond. He swam around a couple of times, and while in the middle of the pond called out to a fellow student on the bank, "Help me, I am drowning!" Arold thought he was joking but when he didn't come back up, he ran for help.

A group of girls, who were friends of Stephany, the boys in the dorm, Michael, my grandson, Richard Comer, a missionary here to hold a Bible conference, and many others watched as Zach Peters, a young man working here from the United States, tried to give CPR to Jaime but to no avail. Finally, he was put on the back of a truck and taken to the doctor's office where he was pronounced dead. We had to look for a casket, dress him in his school uniform, and lay him on a table in the boys dining hall.

I kept watching the clock waiting for his mother to arrive. When she did come, we heard her cries before she entered the building.

She was not a Christian and had no hope of ever seeing Jaime again. A service was held in the dining hall and then his body taken to his home in El Triunfo where he was buried the next day.

Later on I went to visit her. Mario, the pastor, talked with her about the Lord but she did not want to receive Christ as her Saviour.

She showed me her hands, so rough from beating out the dough to make tortillas to sell in the streets. She told me how Jaime had looked at her hands and said, "Mama, one day your hands won't look like this because I will take care of you." She said that only a week or so before, he had asked her where she would go if she died. She answered, "Jaime, don't talk about sad things like that." "It is important, Mama," he said. "I just want you to know that when I die I know that I will go to heaven because I have received Jesus as my Saviour."

She didn't accept the Lord the day we were there but later she came to San Marcos to tell me that she had received the Lord. I already knew about this through the pastor of the church in El Triunfo.

I now sponsor Elvin, who is Jaime's little brother. I feel that by doing this, I am doing something for Jaime.

The next year, another senior in our high school, Nicolle, was killed in a wreck close to our home. She was driving and had lost control of the car when two horses ran out in front of her. Her father, a doctor here in town, was not saved. The mother had left the family and was living in the capital. Her body was brought to the high school auditorium and the funeral preached there.

God used Brother Stan Berrong, co-pastor of Glen Haven Baptist Church in McDonough, Georgia, in a marvelous way, to show love to this grieving family. The Glen Haven group served food to every person who came to the "wake" and showed sincere love and compassion to the grieving parents.

We were told that the mother returned to her husband and family after the funeral.

The deaths of these young people were very hard on our students. It was something that they had never experienced before. Many of them either rededicated their lives to the Lord or received Him in their hearts afterwards. It also made them realize that no matter how old they were or how healthy they were, their lives could be taken away in just an instant. They could be very much alive one second and the next they could be off into eternity. The question was: *where would they spend eternity?* I thank God that as far as we know all three of these teenagers had received Jesus as their Saviour before they died.

Not only were there tragedies but also trials were put before us that we had never experienced when Bob was alive. We lost six pastors in Nicaragua when problems concerning leadership arose. I asked God to give me wisdom and He did. It is not easy to lose someone who has been a part of the family for many years, but as a pastor told me in the United States, "sometimes this is necessary."

Today, two years later, more than 100 pastors in Nicaragua are working together in harmony and with one purpose to win souls for our Lord Jesus Christ. The pastors in Nicaragua have always had an evangelistic spirit, and it is wonderful to hear them make plans to put the tent up in places where the Gospel has never been preached. They all pastor their individual churches but work together in evangelism, going to towns and villages, preaching the Gospel and raising up new churches. Several young preachers from Nicaragua are studying the Bible here in Honduras, and they are sent to pastor these new mission churches.

And so, the work of the Lord is always going forward!

Jesus tells us not to think it strange when the fiery trials come to try us, but it is never easy when we are going through the trials. Thank the Lord, even though sometimes we feel that we are going through this alone, we are never alone.

I Peter 4:13 tells us: "But rejoice, inasmuch as ye are partakers of Christ's suffering, that, when his glory shall be revealed, ye may be glad with exceeding joy."

Bob and I suffered over the years as missionaries, but I don't feel that what little I have suffered could ever be compared to Christ's suffering for me. He left heaven to come to this earth and he suffered—He didn't even have a place to lay his head. He was rejected by men; beaten and scorned by his own creation. Most of all He was nailed to a cross and my sins and the sins of the world were placed upon Him, who knew no sin. God, the father, had to turn his back on Jesus when he was on the cross.

I thank Him every day for what He did for me; one day I will be able to thank Him face to face.

57. A Man Sent From God

Dr. Saul Morel

On March 20, 2004, Stevie wrote the following letter, "In our lives, we know that God works in mysterious ways and many times it is hard to understand His will for our lives."

Stevie's desire was that God would send men who truly loved the radio ministry and with the same desire as he had to see souls saved. At that time, a news program was being sponsored by Dr. Saul Morel, a Christian man, who had medical clinics across the different regions of Honduras.

In 2005, the news program left but Dr. Saul felt led to give free medical consultations over the air to the many needy people that did not have the resources to see a doctor. During this time the radio ministry was going through many transitions because one station was being built after another, and the Lord was opening up new doors every day.

In 2006, when the historic ninth station was being built in the city of Tela, Dr. Saul began to read my first book over the radio. He would take the last 15 or 20 minutes of his program, commenting on the things he had read. In the span of four months the book had been read and people began calling in saying they wanted to be saved. His program became a preaching program and an altar call was given where people could kneel wherever they were and ask the Lord to save them. I have sat at my computer, listening to Dr. Saul over the Internet, and "the hairs on my arms would literally stand," as I listened to this program. As he talked so kind and loving to the callers, asking them to find a place to kneel down and to wait until he finished with the calls and then he would get back to them, my mind went to all the places from where these people could be calling. I could imagine people in their little huts knelt down beside a chair or in a back room beside a hammock or a cot, waiting to pray and ask the Lord to save them.

Dr. Saul would take about 10 minutes before his program closed to pray with the people who were patiently waiting for him to tell them what to do. He would give them the plan of salvation and then ask them to pray and ask Jesus to save them. The phone calls would start coming from all the people who had received the Lord.

He also spent about thirty minutes every day with the children. He would give them assignments, have them to learn Bible verses, ask them Bible questions and have them to call him the next day to answer the questions. It was amazing to hear one call after another from everywhere, even other countries.

In February of 2008 Stevie met with Dr. Saul to see how he could improve the correspondence because approximately 200 phone calls were coming in daily. New equipment was bought for the studios with the purpose of trying to save every possible call. Ninety percent of these calls were about salvation. Dr. Saul was paying for his two-hour program, but the Lord laid it on Stevie's heart to give him thirty more minutes free to be able to extend the invitation. From January 2008 through March of 2009, 11,158 people called in to receive Christ.

On March 7, 2009, Stevie received a call saying that at six o'clock that afternoon our friend and brother, Dr. Saul Morel, had a massive heart attack and passed away. He was found in the office of one of his pharmacies and in his hand was a pen, and in front of him was a notebook. He had been writing the name of every person who had received the Lord that week because every person who called in to be saved was also discipled and Dr. Saul kept a record of every one. He kept a record of every phone call, of every name, and he would call them from his home and encourage them. He freely gave his phone number over the radio for anyone who needed him at whatever hour of the day. At 4:00 am every morning, there was a special prayer time and he asked every radio listener to join him in prayer wherever they were. He had a time of discipleship classes over the radio.

For many of these people, there were no churches close by to attend, and Dr. Saul became their pastor.

We were traveling back from a church service in North Carolina when I received the call from Stevie that Dr. Saul had passed away. He was devastated and kept asking over and over, "Why, Mama? Why would God call Dr. Saul when so many people were being saved? Who will take his place?" My only answer was that God's work does not depend on one person. "God has someone, somewhere to take his place," I told Stevie. Inside, my heart was breaking and I was asking the same question.

Little did we know that God would touch the heart of Dr. Saul's wife and his youngest son to continue his program. They have the same program with the children, answer calls, and play one of Dr. Saul's tapes. It has been a special blessing for me to hear Stevie at times give an invitation at the end of Dr. Saul's tape. And the people still call in to be saved! This is still the most popular program on Samaritan Radio.

I believe with all my heart that Dr. Saul was a man **sent from God** with a definite calling. And when his work on earth was finished, God called him home.

58. Conclusion

There has to be a conclusion to this book, but there is no conclusion to the work of the Lord that is going on here in Honduras, Nicaragua and other places where we serve.

Since God called Bob home on May 20, 2007, there has been a constant growth in the Lord´s work here. Time nor space permits me to name all the new churches that have been established, church buildings that have been constructed, along with pastoriums for the pastors, new Feed the Hungry kitchens built, and new schools opened.

I will never in my lifetime be able to visit all the churches and missions of Good Samaritan Baptist Missions. During the past 40 years, more than 250 churches and missions have been started. National pastors who have been saved in Good Samaritan churches and graduated from the Bible Institute are pastors in all these churches. The Bible Institute which began in Nicaragua continues in Honduras with new preachers graduating every year.

We will never know until we get to Heaven just how many souls Samaritan radio is reaching. God has given us a powerful transmitter in the capital, which alone has the capacity to reach millions—then there are the repeaters in ten other locations.

I am reminded daily of the new life Jesus is giving to the precious old people who are able to eat everyday in the Feed the Elderly kitchen. Someone said the other day, "If these old people don't touch your heart, your heart can´t be touched." It's wonderful just to ride by and see them in their rocking chairs on the front porch of the elderly center, to hear them as they sing "Amazing Grace," and to hear them testify of what Jesus has done for them. Most of them bring little bags, and they'll take a part of their meal home for supper because this is all they will have.

"Opportunity of a Lifetime": This sponsorship program that God laid on our hearts many years ago has changed the lives of thousands. A long time ago, we learned that the only way to help the children and young people in a third world country is to first and foremost see that they have an opportunity to receive the Lord Jesus Christ as Saviour. Secondly, to help them receive an education so that one day they will be able to leave their villages and find work to support themselves and help their families.

"Feed the Hungry" kitchens: This ministry is still making a tremendous difference in the lives of the poor children. We have never changed in more than 25 years the way these kitchens are set up and run. There is still a director from the local church who teaches the Bible every day to the children, they sing and memorize Bible verses—but most important, the children know that Jesus loves them and it is He who sends them the food. I believe this is why this program is blessed and never have we had to close a kitchen because of lack of funds to buy food.

"Christian Schools": Every year we are seeing a growth in the enrollment in our schools. At present we have over 2000 students enrolled in five schools. These children and young people not only receive an excellent education, but also receive Bible classes everyday and a preaching service in Chapel once a week. Hundreds of young people have been saved over the years and have gone into different parts of Honduras and other countries with Jesus in their hearts. We call them "our missionaries."

"REMEMBER HIS MARVELOUS WORKS THAT HE HATH DONE, HIS WONDERS…" —Psalm 105:5.

This is what I have tried to do in writing this book and sharing a few of these marvelous works with you. I trust that you will look at the lives of Bob and Joan Tyson, two very insignificant people who had nothing to offer the Lord but our love and desire to serve Him. If he can do these marvelous works through us, just think what He can do through you if you will turn your life over to Him.

About the Author

Joan Costlow Tyson was born in Taylorsville, Georgia, a small farm community. At the age of twelve, she received the Lord as her personal Saviour in the Taylorsville Baptist Church.

One Sunday morning, a missionary nurse working in Africa spoke to the class, and Joan's heart was touched as she heard about the many boys and girls who knew nothing about Jesus and His love for them. *How exciting,* Joan thought, *to be able to go to a faraway place and tell other girls and boys about Jesus.*

When the missionary gave the class her address, Joan was the first one to write. Anxiously she waited for an answer by the mailbox on the country road. That was over 60 years ago, and she still has the pictures the missionary sent to her.

Joan has always said that Bob's missionary calling was her calling. However, that night in 1965 when Bob told her that God had called him to the mission field, there was reborn in her that same desire that she had experienced many years before when she heard the missionary from Africa speak.

Bob and Joan worked side by side from the beginning. She studied alongside him at Tennessee Temple University. Walking down the aisle together, they received their diplomas. Bob compared their lives and ministry to a pair of oxen, yoked together, with the same purpose—carrying out the Great Commission of the Lord Jesus Christ.

Joan´s life verse:

"Delight thyself also in the Lord; and he shall give thee the desires of thine heart"---Psalm 37.4

"I prayed for one child," Joan says, "and He gave me thousands to love and care for. He has truly given me more than the desires of my heart."

A Tribute To My Husband Bob Tyson

Bob and I were married on July 2, 1954—he was 19 years old, the son of a Baptist preacher. I was 17 years old and had only been out of high school for a few days. Our marriage was rocky in the beginning because I was spoiled and Bob was stubborn. God kept us together because He had a purpose for our lives.

Bob was saved in 1958, while on guard duty in the army, stationed in New Jersey. An immediate change came into his life! He had one desire and that was for others to know this same Jesus that had changed his life. A few months later he was discharged and immediately began working in our home church. We began a new class of young adults and he was elected the teacher. Everything he did, he did with zeal and enthusiasm. In August of 1964 God called him to preach—another turning point in his life. He preached his first message on his 30th birthday, August 10, 1964. Then in October 1964, God had another great plan for Bob's life! He called him to be a missionary. Bob was never the same after that night.

You know the rest of the story. It is written down in this book.

Many thought Bob was a hard man—I knew him as a man of **compassion**. He was hard against sin but he loved the sinner. He had compassion for the poor and would literally give someone the shirt off his back. He was a man of **compassion** who loved lost souls. He had compassion on them because they had never heard, and he wanted them to have an opportunity to be saved. People are still talking about the multitude of poor people who attended his funeral here in Honduras. They came from everywhere. Old people would tell me that Bob brought the Gospel to them—that he baptized them and baptized their children.

He was a **humble** man, something that many didn't see, but I saw it! He never forgot where he came from and where he was when God saved him. He had a humble heart before God.

He was a man with a **forgiving** heart. How many times down through the years did I see him forgive those who had fallen by the way side, including pastors, and Bob picked them up showing Christ's compassion.

He has left a legacy with me as a man of **faith.** He believed that God would provide for His work and God provided—I saw this so many, many times. I would fret sometimes because I did not know where the money was coming from, but then I would see God touch hearts of people that we didn't even know to supply a need.

I saw in Bob a missionary who had received a **divine call** from God. His desire was to go to the next town or the next village where the Gospel had not been preached and he went. I saw him go when he was tired and when he was sick.

—— His work on earth came to an end on May 20, 2007, and he is resting from his labors. Now, we must carry on—his two sons, his grandchildren, and I, along with over 200 preachers and many, many workers whom He left behind. We will work ´**Til' Jesus Comes** ´as the old hymn goes, **and then we'll gather home.**

Photos of the Missionary Journey

Bible Day Parade - Honduras

Front View of the Good Samaritan Tabernacle in Comali, Honduras

Stephany Tyson--school anniversary queen

Bible School, early years, in San Marcos de Colon, Honduras

Bible School, early years, in Condega, Nicaragua

Philadelphia Baptist Church in Vallecillo, Honduras

Bible School Graduation

Ordination of Pastors

Ordination of Pastors

Inside view of the Tabernacle in Comali, Honduras

Outside view of the Good Samaritan Tabernacle

Dedication of Tabernacle

First church established in Palacaguina, Nicaragua in 1970 by Bob Tyson

Samaritan High School boys basketball team- National playoffs

The tent that where Bob Tyson started his ministy

Bob and Joan Tyson ministering in a tent campaign in 1970

Bob Tyson witnessing to the man in the cage

Gilberto the man in the cage after his conversion

Feed the Hungry Children worshiping the Lord

Mt. Calvary Baptist Church in San Marcos de Colon, Honduras

Rev. Ralph Easterwood in Condega, Nicaragua - Steve Tyson translating

Feed the Hungry Center in Comali, Honduras

Elderly Center in San Marcos de Colon, Honduras

Baptism in Honduras

Doves Lifted unto the new Annex

Steve Tyson preaching over the Samaritan Radio Network

Medical Group working in Papalon, Honduras

Good Samaritan Grammar School and Grace Annex - San Marcos de Colon, Honduras

Baptisms in Honduras

Joan Tyson praying with man to receive the Lord as Saviour

Church service-Caire, Honduras

Feed the Hungry Kitchen

Good Samaritan School Children, Condega, Nicaragua

Family of 8 lived in this house in Honduras. They have now been blessed with a better house

Independence Day parade- Students with Bibles

Bob and and Philip Tyson

Good Samaritan Grammar School Graduates

Graduation in La Trinidad, Nicaragua

Dedication of new high school cafeteria

High School Girls Dormitory

Good Samaritan Mission Center, Offices and rooms for groups in Honduras

Motel Rooms for groups in Comali, Honduras

Elderly Kitchen

Feed the Hungry Children

Feed the Hungry Children

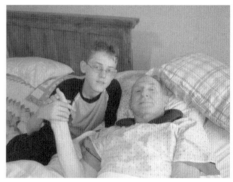
Bob Tyson after surgery with grandson Philip Tyson Jr.

Joan Tyson and son, Stevie

Grammar School children before Annex was built

Birthday Service for Bob Tyson by Honduras National Pastors

Tommy and Mary Lynn Crider

Funeral Services of Bob Tyson in Honduras

Youth Retreat in Honduras with Pastor Rodney Agan

Joan Tyson and Granddaughter, Stephany

Joan Tyson with National Pastors from Nicaragua

School Parade with sign that says "Jesus is our principal teacher"

Old Grammar School building where school first started in 1989

Young people at altar during youth retreat

Bro. Modesto and Petrona, married after living together for 56 years.

Bob and Joan Tyson

High School in Honduras

Good Samaritan High School Students in Honduras

Samaritan School Parade - Independence Day

Samaritan School Parade - Independence Day

Good Samaritan High School

Steve Tyson and Dr. Saul Morel

Bob Tyson